High-Functioning Anxiety

Living With It Without Letting It Run Your Life

Xander Elderfield

First edition, 2026

Published by Xander Elderfield

This book is intended for general educational and reflective purposes only. It is not a substitute for professional financial, legal, medical, or mental health advice, diagnosis, or treatment. Always seek the advice of a qualified professional with any questions regarding your specific circumstances. Never disregard professional advice or delay seeking it because of something you have read in this book. Names and identifying details in any illustrative examples are anonymous/archetypal composites, not depictions of a single real individual.

Contents

Chapter 1: The Invisible Load of Masked Anxiety 1

Chapter 2: Your Body's Early Warning System 25

Chapter 3: Regulation Without Slowing Down 41

Chapter 4: The Performance Trap 61

Chapter 5: Boundaries Without Saying 'No' 83

Chapter 6: Interrupting the Internal Critic 97

Chapter 7: Social Anxiety in Performance Spaces 115

What Your Body Actually Does When It Thinks You're Being Judged 117

The Real Cost of Performing While Your Nervous System Screams 121

The Practice of Watching Yourself Without Dissolving 125

Fast Tools for When Your Heart Is Trying to Escape Your Chest 129

Why Eliminating Anxiety Is the Wrong Goal 135

The Invisible Rules That Keep You Trapped 137

Practicing the Art of Good Enough 139

What Social Anxiety Actually Protects You From (and What It Costs) 143

The Exposure That Actually Works 145

When the Anxiety Is Telling You Something Real 149

Building Your Own Protocol 151

Chapter 8: From Suppression to Expression 153

Chapter 9: Sustaining Regulation Long-Term 171

Also in the Series 191

Chapter 1: The Invisible Load of Masked Anxiety

I prepared for a client presentation by rehearsing it 47 times. I counted because I kept a tally in my notebook—evidence, I told myself, of thoroughness. I slept three hours that night, delivered the presentation "perfectly" according to the feedback (their word, not mine, though I replayed it in my head for validation at least a dozen times afterward), and then sat in my car in the parking garage for twenty minutes, unable to remember if I'd locked my front door that morning.

Not couldn't remember walking through the motion. Couldn't remember *the morning itself.*

That moment—my nervous system finally getting my attention after weeks of override—is when I realized the cost of what I'd been calling "high standards." What I'd been calling excellence. What everyone around me had been rewarding with promotions and praise and the kind of professional currency that makes it almost impossible to question whether you're doing something deeply wrong to yourself.

But let's start somewhere else, because my story isn't the one I want you to see first.

Amelia, a partner at a downtown law firm, is three hours into a negotiation that will determine whether her client keeps or loses a patent worth eight figures. Intellectual property litigation. The opposing counsel is a man twenty years her senior who has a reputation for steamrolling younger attorneys—particularly women—through sheer endurance and condescension. He's been at this since before Amelia graduated high school.

She doesn't steamroll back. She does something quieter and far more effective: she anticipates every single move he makes before he makes it. When he pivots to a contractual argument, she's already got the clause pulled up. When he tries to frame her client's innovation as derivative, she's ready with precedent that undercuts his logic so cleanly he has to pause mid-sentence. She doesn't raise her voice. She doesn't need to. Three hours in, he concedes. Her client is thrilled. Opposing counsel offers a tight, professional handshake that barely conceals his irritation.

Amelia gathers her leather portfolio, her notes (color-coded, cross-referenced, annotated in three different pen colors), her water bottle. She thanks everyone in the room. She walks back to her office with the same measured pace she uses for everything.

It's only when the door clicks shut behind her that she allows her body to do what it's been trying to do for the past three hours.

She doesn't reach for another file. Doesn't open her laptop to draft a follow-up email. She sinks into her chair, closes her eyes, and just... stops. Her shoulders drop so fast it's almost like a collapse. A wave of exhaustion crashes over her—not the tired you feel after a workout, but something deeper, something that makes her bones feel hollow. She's fighting back tears. Not sadness exactly. Just—depletion. The kind that makes you wonder if you'll ever feel rested again.

This happens after every major win. Every high-stakes deposition. Every performance that everyone else sees as evidence of her brilliance.

What Amelia is experiencing isn't ordinary fatigue. It's the crash that comes after suppressing your body's stress response for hours on end. Here's what actually happened inside her during that negotiation:

Her heart rate elevated. Her breathing shallowed. Her muscles tensed—jaw, shoulders, core, even her calves under the table. Adrenaline and cortisol flooded her system, the same chemicals her ancestors produced when facing a predator. Except Amelia wasn't running from a lion. She was sitting in a conference room, appearing calm.

Appearing calm is the key part.

She felt every bit of the activation—the pounding heart, the tight chest, the urge to pace or flee—but she trained herself years ago not to *show* it. To override it. To channel it into hyperfocus and precision. That's what makes her excellent at her job. That's also what's slowly eroding her from the inside.

Because those stress chemicals don't just evaporate when you suppress the outward signs. They stay in your system. The tension doesn't dissolve; it gets stored in muscle tissue. Your nervous system stays activated, stuck in a low-grade fight-or-flight state that never fully resolves. It's like revving a car engine for hours without ever putting it in gear. Everything heats up. Parts wear down faster than they should.

Amelia's body is trying to tell her this. The exhaustion after every win isn't weakness—it's a bill coming due. But she's been taught (by her profession, by her own internal standards, by a culture that celebrates people who "don't let anything faze them") to see it as something to push through. Evidence that she's not working hard enough. Not disciplined enough.

So she pushes harder.

The week after that negotiation, she takes on two more cases. Files motions until midnight. Shows up to her niece's birthday party for exactly forty-three minutes—just long enough to not be the aunt who never shows—and spends most of it checking email in the bathroom. When her sister asks if she's okay, Amelia says she's great. Busy, but great. And she believes it, mostly, because the alternative is admitting that the life she's built is burning her down from the inside.

I need to interrupt the clinical explanation here because I did the same thing. For years. The 47-times rehearsal wasn't an isolated incident—it was my baseline. I didn't see it as anxiety because I didn't have panic attacks. I didn't avoid situations. I walked *into* every high-pressure scenario and performed beautifully. What I didn't do was sleep. Or digest food properly. Or go a single day without my jaw aching from clenching it unconsciously.

I thought I was managing my anxiety. I wasn't. I was just getting really, really good at hiding it from everyone, including myself.

And here's what makes me angry looking back: I wore the exhaustion like a badge. Proof of how hard I was working. How committed I was. I'd mention in passing that I'd only slept four hours, and people would respond with a kind of reverent admiration, like I'd just told them I'd run a marathon before breakfast. The culture I was in—the one most of us are in—treated burnout as a credential.

So I kept earning it.

Let's call this what it actually is: high-functioning anxiety. Which is a term I've grown to resent, honestly, because "high-functioning" makes it sound like something's working well. Like you've figured out how to have anxiety *and* excel, as if that's some kind of sustainable life hack.

It's not high-functioning. It's anxiety that's been trained to look productive.

And the cost? The cost is invisible until suddenly it isn't.

Daniel manages a team of twelve at a software company in Austin. He's forty-two, consistently praised for his calm demeanor under pressure, and has a reputation as the person who never drops a ball. He hits every deadline. He anticipates problems before they escalate. In meetings, he's articulate and measured. His manager describes him as "unflappable."

What his manager doesn't see: Daniel spends an hour every night planning the next day in granular detail. Not just work tasks—he scripts out potential conversations. He rehearses responses to criticism he hasn't received yet. He drafts emails in his head before he writes them, then revises the actual emails four or five times before sending, scanning for anything that could be misinterpreted as unprofessional or, worse, uncertain.

He doesn't experience panic attacks. He's never had a moment where he couldn't breathe or thought he was dying. Instead, he experiences a low-grade hum of tension that lives in his jaw and across his shoulders. He notices it sometimes—usually in the shower, when he's not doing anything else and the tightness becomes impossible to ignore—but he dismisses it. "Just the way I am," he tells himself. Or: "Everyone's stressed at work."

The dismissal is important. Because acknowledging it as *anxiety* would mean admitting he's struggling, and struggling would mean he's not handling things as well as he appears to be, and that gap between appearance and reality is the very thing that terrifies him most.

So he keeps the appearance intact. And the tension builds.

Here's what's happening physiologically: Daniel's nervous system is in a chronic state of threat detection. Not acute panic—chronic activation. His body is perpetually braced for something to go wrong. Muscles stay contracted. His sympathetic nervous system (the "fight or flight" branch) is dominant, which means his parasympathetic nervous system (the "rest and digest" branch) is suppressed.

This isn't just uncomfortable. It has consequences.

His digestion is a mess—bloating, irregular bowel movements, a stomach that feels unsettled more often than not. He gets headaches three or four times a week, usually in the late afternoon. He grinds his teeth at night hard enough that his dentist asked if he's under stress (Daniel said no, reflexively, because admitting stress feels like admitting failure).

And he can't relax. Even on vacation—which he takes reluctantly, because unstructured time feels dangerous—he plans activities meticulously. Hikes scheduled down to the hour. Restaurants researched and reservations made weeks in advance. He tells himself he's being efficient, maximizing the experience. What he's actually doing is maintaining control, because control is the only thing that feels safe.

Letting go, even for a weekend, feels like standing at the edge of a cliff.

Last summer, Daniel's wife suggested they take a spontaneous road trip. No itinerary, just drive up the coast and see where they ended up. He said yes—because he knew that's what a relaxed, fun-loving person would say—but immediately started researching routes on his phone. By the time they left two days later, he had a color-coded spreadsheet with driving times, hotel options, and backup plans in case of traffic.

His wife didn't say anything. She'd learned years ago that fighting it only made him more anxious. But something shifted in her face when she saw the spreadsheet, something Daniel noticed but couldn't bring himself to ask about. A kind of resignation. Like she was watching someone she loved disappear behind a wall she couldn't reach through.

I want to name something here that doesn't get talked about enough: the *belief system* underneath all of this.

People who experience what we're calling high-functioning anxiety aren't just anxious. They're operating under a specific set of rules that make the anxiety feel necessary. Logical, even. The rules sound like this:

- If I don't anticipate every problem, I'll be blindsided and fail. - If I appear uncertain, people will lose respect for me. - If I let my guard down, something bad will happen. - Rest is something you earn after everything is done (and everything is never done). - Needing help is the same as being weak.

These aren't conscious thoughts you'd write in a journal. They're background operating code. And they're reinforced constantly—by a work culture that rewards overperformance, by social media that showcases everyone's highlight reel, by the very real fact that *the vigilance has worked* in tangible ways. Amelia wins cases. Daniel gets promoted. The anxiety looks like it's paying off.

Except it's not the anxiety that's making them successful. It's their competence. Their intelligence. Their actual skills.

The anxiety is just along for the ride, whispering that if they let up for even a second, everything will fall apart.

And here's the thing that makes this pattern so hard to interrupt: the anxiety has been right before. Or at least, it feels like it has. You remember that one time you didn't triple-check something and made a mistake. You remember the presentation where you winged it and stumbled over a question. Your brain catalogs these moments as evidence that vigilance is the only thing standing between you and disaster.

What it doesn't catalog—what it literally can't see—are all the times you would have been fine without the vigilance. All the presentations you could have rehearsed five times instead of forty-seven and still delivered perfectly. All the emails that didn't need four revisions. All the moments where your competence would have carried you even if you hadn't been running on adrenaline and three hours of sleep.

Your brain doesn't collect that data. It only tracks near-misses and failures, real or imagined, and uses them to justify the very pattern that's wearing you down.

Maria is a trial attorney in Chicago. Thirty-eight, known in her firm as unflappable in court. She can think on her feet, handle hostile witnesses, pivot strategy mid-trial without breaking a sweat. She's argued in front of appellate judges who've made younger attorneys cry. She doesn't cry. She doesn't even flinch.

After work, though, she spends hours dissecting her own performance. Not the legal merits—she knows she's good at the law. She replays the *presentation.* Did she hold eye contact long enough with the judge? Was her tone assertive without crossing into aggressive? Did her face betray any emotion when opposing counsel made that low blow about her client's credibility?

She keeps a mental catalogue of every micro-expression, every word choice, every moment where she might have revealed something she didn't intend to reveal. She doesn't share this with anyone. Not her colleagues, who see her as a mentor. Not her partner, who already worries she works too much. Definitely not a therapist, because seeking therapy would mean admitting there's a problem, and admitting a problem feels like handing ammunition to every opposing counsel who's ever tried to undermine her.

So she channels the anxiety into preparation. She overprepares for every case. Researches until 2 a.m. Practices her opening statements in front of a mirror. It works—she wins more than she loses—but the cost is mounting in ways she doesn't connect to the anxiety.

She hasn't slept well in years. She struggles to be present in her relationship; even during dinner, her mind is running through the next day's witness list. She feels perpetually disconnected from herself, like she's watching her own life from a slight distance, performing the role of "successful attorney" without fully inhabiting it.

The word that comes up for her, when she's honest, is *lonely*. Not because she lacks people—she has colleagues, a partner, friends from law school. But because she's never fully *with* anyone. She's always monitoring, editing, managing how she appears.

Her partner asked her once, after a particularly brutal trial, what she was feeling. Not thinking—feeling. And Maria realized she didn't know. She could tell you her strategy for the next day. She could analyze what went wrong in cross-examination. But what she was *feeling*? She'd trained herself so thoroughly to suppress emotional signals that she'd lost access to her own internal experience.

She laughed it off. Said something about being tired. Changed the subject. But the question haunted her for weeks afterward, showing up at odd moments—in the shower, during her commute, in the middle of drafting a motion. *What are you feeling?*

She still doesn't have an answer.

That's the invisible load. It's not just the anxiety itself. It's the constant effort required to conceal it. The monitoring. The performing. The relentless internal surveillance to make sure nothing slips through the carefully constructed facade.

And it's the toll that effort takes on everything else. Your sleep. Your digestion. Your relationships. Your capacity to experience spontaneous joy. Your ability to know what you're actually feeling underneath all the strategy and performance.

You might be thinking: *But I don't have a choice. My job actually does require this level of vigilance. The stakes really are high.*

I hear this a lot, and I want to acknowledge that yes, some professions genuinely demand high performance. Litigation. Surgery. Crisis management. I'm not suggesting you can afford to be careless or unprepared.

But here's the question that matters: Is the level of vigilance you're deploying actually proportional to the stakes? Or have you calibrated your threat-detection system so high that you're treating routine emails like they're life-or-death negotiations?

Because that's what happens with high-functioning anxiety. Your brain loses the ability to distinguish between actual high-stakes situations and routine ones. Everything gets treated as urgent. Everything gets the full-throttle stress response. And you can't sustain that without consequences.

Think about Amelia, running herself into the ground over a negotiation she was *already winning*. She didn't need the three hours of hyperfocused tension to prevail—her skill and preparation had already done that. The anxiety wasn't making her better. It was just making her believe she needed it to survive.

Or Daniel, scripting conversations that would have gone fine without the script. The spreadsheet didn't make the vacation better—it made it tolerable for his nervous system, but at the cost of the spontaneity his wife was hoping for, the kind that actually restores you.

The vigilance starts as a tool. Then it becomes a habit. Then it becomes the only way you know how to function. And by that point, you can't tell the difference between the competence that makes you good at your job and the anxiety that's just tagging along, demanding credit.

Let me tell you what happened after the parking garage incident, after I finally realized what I'd been doing to myself.

I didn't immediately quit my job or have some dramatic breakdown. I just started paying attention to the cost. I started asking myself: *What am I sacrificing to maintain this appearance of having it all together?*

The answer was: almost everything that mattered.

I was sacrificing sleep, obviously. Physical health—my stomach was a disaster, and I'd normalized that as "just how my body is." I was sacrificing presence with the people I loved, because even when I was physically there, I was mentally rehearsing something else. I was sacrificing joy. Actual, spontaneous joy. Because joy requires a kind of unselfconsciousness that I hadn't allowed myself in years.

And here's the thing that made me angriest: I was sacrificing all of this *voluntarily*. No one was holding a gun to my head demanding I rehearse a presentation 47 times. I was doing it to myself, in service of a standard that no one else was even holding me to.

The perfectionism, the hypervigilance, the relentless self-monitoring—I thought those were the *source* of my success. And maybe they were, early on. But they'd long since crossed the line from helpful into destructive, and I'd been too busy performing competence to notice.

I started doing something that felt almost transgressive at the time: I started experimenting with doing less.

Not performing worse. Just... doing less of the invisible preparation that no one saw anyway.

I rehearsed a presentation five times instead of forty-seven. I revised an email once instead of four times. I went to a dinner party without pre-scripting conversation topics in my head.

And you know what happened? Nothing. No disasters. No failures. No one looked at me differently or questioned my competence. The presentations went fine. The emails were clear. The conversations flowed.

The only thing that changed was how I felt afterward. Instead of depleted, I was just... tired. Normal tired. The kind you recover from with a good night's sleep.

It was such a small shift, but it cracked something open. Because if I could do less and still be fine—if the catastrophe I'd been guarding against all those years didn't actually materialize when I lowered my guard—then what had I been doing to myself all this time?

So let's talk about what this looks like in the body, because understanding the physiology helps make it real. And because your body is where the cost shows up first, long before you're ready to admit there's a problem.

Chronic muscle tension is probably the most common physical manifestation. Not the dramatic clenching you'd experience if someone jumped out and scared you—this is subtler. A baseline tightness that becomes so familiar you stop noticing it's there.

Your shoulders ride higher than they need to. Your jaw is set just slightly too firm. You might brace your core without realizing it, holding your abdomen tight as if preparing for impact. Over time, this becomes your default state.

And it's *expensive*, metabolically. Holding muscles in a contracted state requires energy. Real, measurable energy expenditure. Your body is working overtime to maintain this level of readiness, which means resources get diverted from other essential functions. Like digestion. Like immune response. Like cellular repair.

David—one of Daniel's colleagues, actually, a software architect with the same unflappable reputation—described feeling "wired but tired." Always running, but never rested. That phrase stuck with me because it's so precise. His body was burning through energy maintaining a state of high alert, but that kind of activation doesn't produce the restorative rest he actually needed.

He came to me initially for help with insomnia, which he attributed to work stress. But the insomnia wasn't separate from the anxiety—it was a symptom of the same underlying pattern. His nervous system couldn't downshift. Even when he was lying in bed, supposedly resting, his mind was running through the next day's agenda, anticipating problems, rehearsing solutions.

Sleep requires your body to shift into parasympathetic mode—the rest-and-digest state. But David's system was stuck in sympathetic dominance. The engine was always running. Falling asleep felt impossible, not because he wasn't tired (he was exhausted), but because his body didn't feel *safe* enough to let go.

Here's what he told me that I'll never forget: "I lie there thinking about how I need to sleep because I have a big day tomorrow, which makes me more anxious about not sleeping, which makes it even harder to fall asleep. And the whole time I'm judging myself for not being able to do something as basic as rest."

The anxiety about the anxiety. That's the recursion that traps you.

The gut issues are harder to dismiss once you understand the mechanism.

Your digestive system is intricately wired to your nervous system through the vagus nerve. When you're in a state of chronic activation—when your body believes, on some level, that you're under threat—it diverts blood flow and energy away from digestion. Why waste resources breaking down food when you might need to fight or flee?

Except you're not actually fleeing. You're sitting at a desk, or in a meeting, or arguing a case. But your body doesn't know the difference between a physical predator and a psychological threat. A looming deadline activates the same stress response as a lion chasing you across the savannah. And in both cases, digestion shuts down.

Sarah, a marketing executive I worked with, was convinced for *years* that she had a food allergy. She kept meticulous food diaries. Eliminated gluten, dairy, soy, nightshades—anything anyone suggested might be causing her bloating and abdominal pain. Nothing helped.

It wasn't until she started addressing the underlying anxiety that the digestive issues began to improve. Not because anxiety was "all in her head" (I hate that phrase—it dismisses real suffering). But because the anxiety was *in her body*, actively disrupting her gut function.

She was striving for perfection in every domain of her life. Flawless presentations at work. A spotless home. A curated social media presence. Thoughtful gifts for every occasion. She didn't see this as anxiety—she saw it as being conscientious, reliable, someone people could count on.

But her body was keeping score. The constant pressure she put on herself translated into chronic tension, which translated into a chronically compromised digestive system. Her "allergy" wasn't about what she was eating. It was about how her nervous system was responding to the relentless demand for perfection.

The thing is, Sarah had seen doctors. Multiple specialists. Had expensive tests. Tried every elimination diet and probiotic on the market. She'd spent thousands of dollars and countless hours trying to fix the problem from the outside, never considering that the source might be the way she was living her entire life.

When I suggested this connection, she was skeptical. Understandably. Because accepting that her gut issues were related to her anxiety meant accepting that her approach to life—the very things that made her successful and admired—was hurting her. That's a hard pill to swallow.

But she was desperate enough to try. She started small. Stopped checking work email after 8 p.m. Let her house be messy for a week without spiraling. Said no to hosting Thanksgiving, something she'd done for a decade but secretly dreaded.

Within three weeks, her digestion started to normalize. Not perfectly—it took months of sustained change—but noticeably. Enough that she couldn't dismiss the connection anymore.

Here's the part that makes this pattern so insidious: it's incredibly hard to recognize from the inside.

Because high-functioning anxiety doesn't look like dysfunction. It looks like success. It gets rewarded—with promotions, praise, increased responsibility. People tell you you're "so good under pressure" or "always so calm and collected," and those compliments reinforce the very behavior that's draining you.

You're not avoiding things. You're showing up. Performing. Delivering. So how could it be a problem?

The problem is the *cost* that no one sees. The cost you're paying in your body, in your sleep, in your ability to be present with the people you love, in your capacity for joy.

And because the cost is invisible—hidden beneath the polished exterior—it's easy to dismiss. Easy to tell yourself you're just busy, just stressed, just need to power through. Easy to believe that if you could just be a little more disciplined, a little more organized, a little more *on top of things*, the exhaustion would resolve itself.

It won't. Because the exhaustion isn't from doing too much. It's from never allowing your nervous system to fully rest.

Here's what I mean by that. Normal stress—the kind that comes from an actual challenge—has a rhythm to it. There's activation (you encounter the challenge), mobilization (you meet it), and then resolution (you rest afterward). Your nervous system is designed for this rhythm. It can handle intense activation as long as there's recovery on the other side.

But high-functioning anxiety doesn't follow that rhythm. There's activation without resolution. Your body revs up to meet the challenge, then stays revved. You move from one high-stakes situation to the next without ever fully coming down. The stress response that's supposed to be temporary becomes chronic.

And chronic activation wears everything down. Your adrenal system. Your immune function. Your capacity to regulate emotion. Your ability to experience pleasure from things that used to bring you joy.

That last one is worth sitting with. When was the last time you felt uncomplicated happiness? Not relief that something went well. Not satisfaction from checking something off your list. Just... joy. The unselfconscious kind that doesn't require anything from you.

If you can't remember, that's a sign. Not that you're broken, but that you've been running your nervous system so hard for so long that it's forgotten how to rest.

Let me offer you something practical here, because I know your brain (especially if it works like mine) is already asking: *Okay, but what do I do about this?*

First, I want you to notice that impulse. The one that just skipped straight from recognizing the problem to demanding a solution. That's the same pattern we're talking about. The same one that won't let you sit with discomfort or uncertainty for even a moment before mobilizing to fix it.

So before I give you anything to *do*, I want you to try something that's going to feel insufficient and possibly pointless. But I promise it's not.

For the next three days, once a day, I want you to check in with your body. Not to change anything. Not to fix anything. Just to notice what's there.

Set a timer for three minutes. You can do this at your desk, in your car, wherever. Close your eyes if that feels okay, or just soften your gaze.

Start with your feet. Just bring your attention there. Notice the pressure where they touch the floor. The temperature. Any sensation at all—tingling, numbness, warmth, tightness. You're not trying to make anything happen. Just noticing.

Then move up. Calves. Thighs. Hips. Spend a few seconds with each area, just checking: *What's here?*

Abdomen. Chest. Notice the rhythm of your breath without trying to control it.

Shoulders. Neck. Jaw. These are places where tension lives for most people, so you might notice tightness. That's fine. You're not trying to relax it. Just acknowledging: *Oh, there's tension here.*

Then let your attention rest on your whole body for a moment. Just sitting here. Breathing. Existing.

That's it. Three minutes. Once a day for three days.

I know this sounds too simple to matter. Your brain probably wants a more sophisticated intervention—a structured program, a set of techniques, something that feels proportional to the size of the problem.

But here's what's actually happening when you do this: You're practicing noticing sensation without immediately trying to fix it. You're building the capacity to be *with* your experience instead of constantly managing it.

That capacity—the ability to tolerate what's happening in your body without needing to change it right away—is the foundation for everything else. Because you can't regulate a nervous system you're not even aware of. And you can't shift a pattern you haven't learned to recognize.

So start there. Three minutes. Notice what's present.

If you do this for three days and it feels like a waste of time, fine. You've lost nine minutes. But if you do it and you start to notice patterns—places where tension lives that you'd stopped registering, moments where your breath is shallower than you realized—then you've gained something more valuable than any technique I could give you. You've gained awareness. And awareness is where change actually begins.

Let me tell you what I noticed when I started doing this myself, back when I was still in the parking-garage-can't-remember-my-morning phase of my life.

The first day, I felt almost nothing. Or I felt sensations, but they didn't mean anything to me. My mind kept wandering to my to-do list. I had to restart the timer twice because I got distracted.

The second day, I noticed my jaw was clenched. I'd been clenching it so long it felt normal, but when I brought my attention there, I realized it was *tight*. Like, painfully tight. I hadn't registered it as pain before because I'd trained myself to ignore low-level discomfort.

The third day—and this is the one that broke something open—I noticed that my chest felt heavy. Not in a medical emergency way. Just... dense. Like there was pressure sitting on my sternum. And when I stayed with that sensation instead of immediately distracting myself, I realized it was grief.

Not grief about anything specific. Just a baseline sadness that I'd been carrying around without acknowledging. Sadness about how hard I'd been pushing myself. About all the things I was missing while I was busy performing competence. About the version of myself I'd abandoned in favor of the version everyone else praised.

I cried in my car that day. Not the dramatic sobbing kind of crying—just tears, quiet and unexpected. And afterward, I felt lighter. Not fixed. Not healed. Just... less heavy.

That's what happens when you stop managing your experience long enough to actually feel it. The feelings don't destroy you. They move through you. And on the other side, there's space for something else.

So here's what I want you to understand about the invisible load you've been carrying:

It's not a sign of strength. It's a sign of a nervous system that never learned it was safe to rest.

It's not making you better at your job. It's making you believe you need it to survive your job, which is not the same thing.

It's costing you more than you realize—not just in sleep and digestion and physical health, but in presence, in connection, in your ability to inhabit your own life instead of just performing it.

And most importantly: You don't have to live this way.

Not because there's something wrong with you for living this way now. But because there's another option. One where you bring the same competence and intelligence and care to your work, but without the underlying hum of chronic activation. Where you can meet high-stakes situations when they actually arise, then come back down afterward. Where rest isn't something you have to earn—it's just part of the rhythm.

That option exists. It's not easy to get there, and it doesn't happen overnight. But it starts with recognizing the cost. With naming the pattern. With admitting that what you've been calling "high-functioning" is just anxiety in a really convincing disguise.

You've been running the engine at redline for so long you've forgotten there are other speeds. Your body hasn't forgotten, though. It's been trying to tell you, in the tightness in your jaw and the exhaustion after every win and the stomach that won't settle and the sleep that won't come.

The question now is: Are you ready to listen?

Not to fix it immediately. Not to add "address anxiety" to your already overwhelming to-do list. Just to listen. To acknowledge what's true. To stop dismissing the signals your body has been sending and start treating them as the valuable information they are.

Because that acknowledgment—that simple act of recognizing the invisible load you've been carrying—is the first step toward setting it down.

And in the next chapter, we're going to talk about what those signals actually mean. How your body communicates stress in ways that are easy to miss or dismiss. How to distinguish between the activation that serves you and the activation that's just running on autopilot, burning resources you can't afford to waste.

But for now, just sit with this: The exhaustion you feel isn't a personal failing. It's not evidence that you're not working hard enough or that you need better time management or more discipline.

It's your body trying to tell you something that your mind hasn't been willing to hear.

What if, just for a moment, you listened?

Chapter 2: Your Body's Early Warning System

I first noticed it during a family dinner about two years ago. My sister—halfway through her pasta—put down her fork and looked at me. "Are you okay? You seem tense."

I smiled immediately. "I'm great!" The words came out too bright, too automatic.

The truth? My jaw was locked so tight I could barely chew. I'd been grinding my teeth through the entire meal without noticing, my body screaming while I performed ease. I caught myself later that night, standing in my bathroom, jaw still clenched, and thought: *How long have I been doing this?*

That's the thing about high-functioning anxiety. It doesn't announce itself. It doesn't derail your day or send you home early from work. It just…hums. A low-grade static beneath everything you do. And your body? Your body picks up the signal long before your mind admits there's a problem.

*

Imagine this. You're preparing for a presentation at work. The slides are polished. Talking points memorized. Outfit chosen down to the socks. From the outside, you look composed—confident, even. But as you run through your opening lines one more time, you notice something: your jaw is locked tight. Not a conscious clench. Just…held. Your breathing? Short, shallow puffs that barely expand your chest.

You smooth your blouse. Adjust your glasses. Anything to avoid acknowledging what's happening *inside*.

You tell yourself everyone feels this way before a presentation. It's just nerves. Normal. And sure enough, you deliver flawlessly. The jaw ache lingers for hours afterward, though. That shallow breathing becomes a pattern throughout the week—during emails, during meetings, even while relaxing at home.

This isn't nerves. This is your body's early warning system, and most of us have learned to ignore it so thoroughly we don't even register the alarms anymore.

*

Here's what we get wrong about anxiety: we think of it as a mental experience. Racing thoughts. Catastrophic predictions. Worry spirals that keep us up at night. And yes, that's part of it. But that's the smoke, not the fire.

The fire starts in your body.

Your nervous system doesn't wait for your conscious mind to catch up. It's designed for survival, and its job is to detect threats *before* you're aware of them. When your ancestors faced a predator or a hostile tribe, the body didn't pause to deliberate. It acted. Adrenaline surged. Muscles tensed. Breathing quickened. Digestion slowed. Everything optimized for fight or flight.

The problem isn't that these responses are wrong. It's that your brain sometimes misinterprets a demanding boss, a looming deadline, or a critical email as a life-or-death emergency. And the signals it sends? They're often subtle. A tightening in your chest when you open your inbox. A slight tremor in your hands during a phone call.

Persistent shoulder tension at the end of the day.

These are the earliest indicators. The quiet alarms. And they're so ingrained, we barely register them anymore. They just *are*.

I'll be honest: I spent years dismissing mine. The jaw clenching? "I'm just focused." The tight shoulders? "Everyone who works at a desk gets those." The knot in my stomach before difficult conversations? "That's normal." I had an explanation for everything, and none of them involved the word *anxiety* because anxiety meant falling apart, and I was fine. Look how much I was getting done.

Except I wasn't fine. I was just really, *really* good at performing fine.

*

Let me tell you about David.

He's a lawyer—successful, respected, known for his calm demeanor in court. When opposing counsel tried to rattle him, he didn't flinch. He thought on his feet. Colleagues admired his composure.

What they didn't see was the constant static beneath it.

For years, David carried a dull ache across his upper back that radiated around to his ribs. His stomach knotted whenever he had to deliver bad news to a client. He told himself this was just the job—high-stakes work comes with stress. Occupational hazard.

But this wasn't simply stress. This was his system perpetually braced for impact. His body was anticipating conflict even when there was no immediate danger. The muscle tension became chronic, triggering migraines that knocked him flat for entire weekends. His sleep deteriorated. He'd wake up exhausted, jaw sore from grinding his teeth all night.

David didn't realize he could actually *do* something about it. He thought this was just how his body worked. The cost of being good at what he did.

And that's the insidious part, isn't it? We rationalize. We normalize. We tell ourselves everyone feels this way, and maybe they do, but that doesn't mean we should just…endure it.

Because here's what chronic activation actually costs you: energy. Creativity. The ability to be present with the people you love. You think you're managing it, keeping all the plates spinning, but you're bleeding resources you didn't even know you had. Your immune system takes a hit. Your digestion falls apart. You get sick more often, recover more slowly. Sleep stops being restorative. And the kicker? You start believing this is just who you are—someone who's "always been anxious," someone who "just runs hot."

It's not who you are. It's what's happening to you while you're too busy performing competence to notice.

*

So what's actually happening when anxiety kicks in?

Your sympathetic nervous system—the part responsible for fight-or-flight—ramps up. This triggers the release of cortisol and adrenaline. Your heart rate increases. Blood pressure rises. Breathing becomes faster and shallower. Blood flow shifts away from non-essential functions like digestion and toward your muscles and vital organs. It's a real, measurable cascade of events.

But it's not just hormones. The brain plays a huge role too.

The amygdala—often called the fear center—processes emotional stimuli. When it perceives a threat, it sends signals to other parts of the brain, including the prefrontal cortex, which handles higher-level thinking and decision-making. In high-functioning anxiety, this circuit becomes hyperactive. You're not necessarily *feeling* terrified. You're just operating in a state of low-grade apprehension. A persistent sense that something bad might happen.

And your body responds accordingly. Constantly. For years.

This ongoing activation takes a toll. Chronic muscle tension leads to pain, headaches, fatigue. Shallow breathing restricts oxygen flow, impacting energy levels and cognitive function. Digestive issues become common as blood is diverted away from the gut. Over time, this constant state of stress contributes to more serious health problems—not because you're weak or broken, but because your system was never designed to run at this level indefinitely.

The key isn't to eliminate anxiety entirely. That's neither possible nor desirable. A little nervousness can sharpen focus, enhance performance. It's when the system gets *stuck* in chronic activation—when those subtle signals escalate into overwhelming symptoms—that it becomes a problem.

And learning to decode those signals? That's the first step toward regaining control.

*

Let's start with the jaw.

For many people, high-functioning anxiety manifests as persistent tightness there—sometimes so ingrained they barely notice until someone points it out. This isn't just "stress." It's your body bracing.

Think about what happens when you anticipate a physical impact. A ball coming toward you. A stumble. Your jaw instinctively clenches, preparing for the force. With chronic anxiety, that preparation becomes…well, chronic.

Your mind doesn't differentiate between an actual threat and perceived pressure—a looming deadline, a difficult conversation, even just the weight of expectation. It sends signals to tense muscles throughout your body, and the jaw is often one of the first places this happens because of its proximity to facial expression and communication. We subtly "armor up" for potential social discomfort.

What's actually happening isn't random. It's a feedback loop driven by the sympathetic nervous system. When you perceive a threat—real or imagined—adrenaline surges, increasing muscle tension. That tension, if sustained, restricts blood flow and can lead to headaches, facial pain, even temporomandibular joint (TMJ) issues.

But focusing on *treating* those symptoms misses the point. The jaw clenching isn't the problem. It's a messenger. Your body saying, "Hey, something feels unsafe here."

A simple regulation tool is focused release. Throughout the day, intentionally scan for tension in your jaw. Gently separate your teeth—don't force it—and let your tongue rest flat on the roof of your mouth. You can add a slow, deliberate exhale while doing this.

It's not about eliminating the clenching entirely. That would be unrealistic and probably counterproductive. It's about interrupting the constant state of tension. Reminding your nervous system it doesn't *always* need to be braced for impact.

Amelia, a project manager I know, prides herself on meticulous planning. What others see as organization, she feels as relentless pressure. During meetings—even routine updates—her jaw would lock tight. She hadn't consciously registered it as discomfort. She just assumed it was concentration.

Then one day, a colleague casually mentioned she looked "a bit strained."

That comment landed differently than it should have. Amelia went home that night and stood in front of her bathroom mirror, and for the first time, she actually *looked.* Her jaw was clenched. Her shoulders were up around her ears. She looked like she was waiting for something to hit her.

She started practicing the focused release technique—separating her teeth and breathing deeply for a few moments. It didn't magically dissolve her anxiety. But it *did* create a small pocket of calm in what otherwise felt like constant overdrive. She incorporated this little reset throughout her workday—during email, while reviewing reports, even during brief pauses between calls.

The clenching didn't disappear. But it became less pervasive. Less automatic. It was as though she'd given herself permission to *not* be constantly on guard.

*

Then there's the breath.

Shallow breathing—rapid, chest-focused inhales and exhales—is another classic sign of heightened anxiety. And again, this isn't a character flaw. It's physiology.

When you feel threatened, your body prepares for fight or flight. One crucial element of that preparation is shifting blood flow away from non-essential functions like digestion and toward your muscles in anticipation of physical exertion. As a result, breathing becomes faster and shallower, delivering more oxygen to those muscles.

It's efficient...if you're about to run from a predator. But if you're sitting at a desk answering emails, it just leaves you feeling wired and depleted.

The problem isn't that your breath *can* become shallow. It's that it often *stays* that way. Your nervous system gets stuck in this heightened state even when there's no immediate threat. You might not consciously realize how restricted your breathing is—it becomes the new normal. And because oxygen deprivation subtly impacts cognitive function, it can actually exacerbate anxiety, creating a vicious cycle: anxiety causes shallow breathing, which worsens anxiety.

A regulation tool here is diaphragmatic breathing—belly breathing. It sounds simple, and it is, but it requires conscious effort to override years of ingrained patterns.

Place one hand on your chest and the other on your abdomen. Inhale slowly through your nose, focusing on expanding your *belly* rather than lifting your chest. You should feel your lower hand rise more noticeably than your upper hand. Exhale slowly through your mouth, allowing your belly to fall.

It feels strange at first. We're rarely taught to breathe this way. But it activates the parasympathetic nervous system—the "rest and digest" system—helping to slow your heart rate, lower blood pressure, and calm your mind.

David—the lawyer I mentioned earlier—experienced persistent anxiety about making mistakes. Not necessarily losing cases, but failing to anticipate every possible objection or nuance. This worry manifested as almost constant breath-holding during focused work. He'd realize hours later he hadn't taken a full, deep breath all afternoon.

When he started practicing diaphragmatic breathing, it felt incredibly awkward. His chest would instinctively rise first, and his abdomen felt resistant to expanding. But he persisted, setting reminders on his phone to check in with his breath throughout the day. He wasn't aiming for perfection—just awareness.

Over time, belly breathing became more natural. It created moments of genuine calm amidst the pressure of his work. It didn't eliminate his anxiety entirely, but it gave him a tangible tool to regulate his physical response when he felt overwhelmed.

(And honestly? I had the same experience. The first time I tried belly breathing, I felt ridiculous. Like I was doing it wrong, even though there's no "wrong" way to breathe. I kept thinking, *This can't possibly work.* But I was desperate enough to try it anyway, and what I noticed wasn't some profound shift—it was just...a loosening. A tiny bit of space between me and the static.)

*

Finally, let's talk about stomach upset.

Nausea. Indigestion. Irritable bowel syndrome. These aren't always signs of food sensitivities or digestive disorders. They can be powerful indicators of underlying anxiety.

Remember that shift in blood flow during the fight-or-flight response? Digestion is one of the first systems to shut down. Blood and energy are diverted toward more immediate survival needs. This isn't a judgment. It's biology.

The problem arises when this happens repeatedly, leaving your digestive system chronically underfunded. It can disrupt gut bacteria, impair nutrient absorption, and contribute to inflammation. And here's where things get particularly tricky: the gut and brain are intimately connected via the vagus nerve—often referred to as the "gut-brain axis." Inflammation in the gut can send signals to the brain that exacerbate anxiety, creating another vicious cycle.

A useful regulation tool is mindful eating. This isn't about dieting or restricting food groups. It's about approaching meals with intention and awareness.

Slow down. Chew your food thoroughly. Pay attention to the taste, texture, and smell. Turn off distractions—put away your phone, turn off the TV.

It sounds simple, but in our fast-paced world, it's revolutionary. By slowing down and engaging all your senses, you activate the parasympathetic nervous system, signaling to your body that it's safe to digest.

Elena is a graphic designer who masked her anxiety with relentless productivity. She routinely ate lunch at her desk while working, barely tasting her food. She described it as "fueling up."

Eventually, she developed chronic bloating and indigestion. A friend suggested mindful eating. Elena initially resisted—she didn't have *time* to sit and savor a meal. But she agreed to try it for one week.

It was surprisingly difficult. Her mind raced with thoughts about deadlines and projects. She kept wanting to multitask. But slowly, she began to notice the subtle flavors of her food. She felt herself relaxing.

The bloating didn't disappear overnight. But it gradually lessened as her digestive system regained some functionality. Mindful eating wasn't a cure for her anxiety. It was a way to reconnect with her body and soothe a chronically stressed nervous system.

*

You might be thinking: *Okay, but these techniques seem so small. How is separating my teeth or eating more slowly supposed to fix anxiety?*

Fair question. And the answer is: they won't. Not by themselves.

These aren't fixes. They're interventions. They're ways to interrupt the cycle of chronic activation *before* it escalates. Think of them as circuit breakers—not rewiring the whole house, just preventing the system from overloading.

The jaw clenching, the shallow breathing, the digestive upset—these are just three examples of how your body communicates distress. There are countless others. The key isn't memorizing a list of symptoms. It's cultivating an ongoing dialogue with your own physiology.

What does *your* body tell you when you're overwhelmed? Where do you first feel the tension building?

For some people, it's a tightness in the chest. For others, it's a heaviness in the limbs. Some people get headaches. Some people's hands go cold. Some people feel a buzzing sensation, like their nervous system is vibrating at a frequency slightly too high.

The signals are different for everyone. But they're there. And paying attention to them—really paying attention, not just acknowledging and dismissing—gives you something most of us don't have: *lead time*.

Because here's the truth: by the time anxiety reaches your conscious awareness as a thought ("I'm anxious"), your body has already been responding for minutes, maybe hours. Your nervous system detected the threat—real or imagined—and began preparing you to deal with it. The physical cascade was already underway.

But if you can catch those early signals—the jaw clenching, the breath shortening, the stomach tightening—you can intervene before the full-blown response takes over. You can interrupt the feedback loop. You can remind your system that it's safe, that it doesn't need to stay on high alert indefinitely.

This isn't about achieving some mythical state of permanent calm. It's about building the capacity to regulate yourself when things get hard. It's about recognizing that anxiety isn't a character flaw or a sign of weakness—it's a physiological process with very real consequences, and like any physiological process, it can be influenced.

*

Mark was a project manager who described himself as "always on." If you asked how things were going, he'd launch into detailed updates, meticulously covering every potential problem and contingency plan—a habit that felt productive but left him exhausted at the end of each day.

What Mark hadn't connected was the subtle physical cascade happening beneath his relentless planning.

First, it was just a persistent tightness in his jaw—something he attributed to needing new glasses or maybe clenching while concentrating. Then came the digestive issues, easily dismissed as "just stress" from long hours. He'd also begun grinding his teeth at night, which his partner pointed out.

These weren't isolated incidents. They were escalating signals that his system was stuck in a heightened state of alert.

The jaw tension was his initial muscular response to perceived threat—a preparing-to-speak, prepare-to-fight posture. The digestive upset reflected blood being diverted away from non-essential functions and toward muscle preparedness. The teeth grinding? Pure, unconscious physical release of accumulated tension when he wasn't actively managing things in his mind.

The difference between a helpful alert and an escalating alarm is often about intensity and duration. A brief surge of adrenaline before a presentation can sharpen focus and improve performance. That's adaptive anxiety at work.

But when that same physiological response becomes chronic—when your muscles are consistently tense, your heart rate elevated, your digestive system erratic—it depletes your resources and impairs your ability to function effectively. It's the difference between preparing for a sprint and being perpetually poised on the starting blocks.

Recognizing that tipping point is crucial, but it requires practice. We're often so accustomed to ignoring or minimizing these early signals that they become normalized until they reach a critical level.

Think of it like a slow leak in a tire. Initially, you might not even notice the pressure dropping. But if you continue driving without addressing it, eventually the tire will fail catastrophically.

Sarah, an architect, presented similarly to Mark: outwardly calm and capable, inwardly consumed by worry about project details. She wouldn't experience panic. Her anxiety manifested as a constant feeling of being "wired but tired."

Her early warning sign was subtle—a persistent warmth in her chest that she initially dismissed as heartburn. It wasn't pain, just…*presence*. She'd also noticed an increase in the frequency of needing to urinate, which she chalked up to drinking too much coffee.

What Sarah hadn't realized was that the warmth in her chest was actually a localized sensation of increased blood flow—her heart subtly pumping harder as her sympathetic nervous system geared up for action. The frequent urination wasn't simply caffeine. It reflected the body attempting to regulate itself, shedding excess fluids and metabolic byproducts released during heightened arousal.

When I asked her to pay attention to *when* these sensations arose, she began noticing a pattern: they coincided with deadlines, client meetings, or any situation where she felt responsible for delivering a perfect outcome.

She started using a simple body scan exercise—briefly checking in with herself throughout the day, noticing any areas of tension or discomfort—to identify these early signals. It wasn't about *stopping* the feeling. It was about acknowledging it without judgment.

And that acknowledgment? That's where the shift begins.

*

Here's what I want you to do right now.

Put this book down for a moment. Close your eyes. Take a slow breath in through your nose—count to four. Hold it for a second. Exhale through your mouth—count to six.

Now scan your body from head to toe. Where are you holding tension? Is your jaw clenched? Are your shoulders up by your ears? Is your stomach tight? Are your hands balled into fists?

Don't try to fix anything. Just notice.

Because the body you've been ignoring—the one that's been sending you signals for months, maybe years—is still talking. And it's not going to stop until you start listening.

The question is: what is it trying to tell you?

Chapter 3: Regulation Without Slowing Down

I was in the middle of a work presentation when it happened. Heart racing, palms sweating, that familiar tightness creeping across my chest. I could see my manager in the front row, nodding along, completely oblivious. Afterward, she pulled me aside. "You seemed a little tense up there," she said, her voice all concern and good intentions. "Next time, just take a few deep breaths before you start. It really helps."

Just breathe.

I smiled. Nodded. Thanked her for the advice. And inside, I wanted to scream.

Because here's what she didn't understand: I had been breathing. I'd been doing the breathing exercises my therapist taught me. I'd been practicing mindfulness. I'd downloaded three different meditation apps. And none of it had stopped my body from lighting up like a fire alarm the moment I stood in front of that room.

The problem wasn't that I didn't know how to breathe. The problem was that "just breathing" felt like being handed a garden hose to fight a wildfire.

Most anxiety advice is built for people whose anxiety looks like what anxiety is supposed to look like—visible panic, obvious distress, someone who needs to calm down because they've clearly lost control. But high-functioning anxiety doesn't work that way. You're already in control. You're holding it together. You're breathing just fine, thank you very much, even as your nervous system runs a silent marathon underneath your composed exterior.

And that's exactly why the standard toolkit falls short.

Think about the last time someone offered you one of those classic anxiety interventions. Deep breathing. Progressive muscle relaxation. Visualization. Maybe even a gratitude journal. These aren't bad tools—I'm not here to trash perfectly legitimate techniques. But when you're already operating at capacity, when you're already doing seventeen things at once while appearing perfectly calm, being told to add another practice to your routine feels less like support and more like one more thing you're failing at.

I remember sitting in a workshop on stress management—ironic, I know—where the facilitator had us all lie on yoga mats for a twenty-minute guided body scan. Around me, people were sighing, settling in, presumably releasing their tension into the universe. And me? I was mentally rewriting my presentation for the afternoon, running through my to-do list, calculating whether I'd have time to grab lunch, and silently berating myself for not being able to just relax like everyone else.

The facilitator's voice drifted over us: "Notice any areas of tension... and simply let them go."

Simply.

That word haunted me for weeks. Because nothing about it felt simple. The tension in my shoulders wasn't something I could just "let go" any more than I could let go of gravity. It was woven into how I moved through the world—a constant bracing for whatever came next.

What I've learned since then is this: high-functioning anxiety doesn't need you to stop. It needs you to move differently.

The tools that actually work aren't about achieving some state of zen-like calm. They're not about emptying your mind or finding your center or any of the other things that sound lovely in theory but feel impossible in practice. They're about working with your nervous system instead of against it. About making micro-adjustments that don't require you to step out of your life to implement them.

Let me tell you what this looks like in real terms.

There's a reason traditional deep breathing sometimes backfires for people like us. When your nervous system is already hypervigilant, when you're already scanning for threats and monitoring every internal sensation, focusing intently on your breath can paradoxically increase anxiety. You become hyperaware of every inhale and exhale. You start wondering if you're doing it right. Whether you're breathing too fast or too slow. Whether this is even working or if you're just adding "can't breathe properly" to your list of inadequacies.

I've seen this play out dozens of times. Clients who come in frustrated because meditation makes them more anxious, not less. Who feel like failures because they can't seem to get the one thing that's supposed to work for everyone.

But you're not failing. The tool just wasn't designed for how your nervous system operates.

What works better is what I call tactile grounding—deliberately shifting your attention to physical sensation. Not your breath, which carries all this weight and expectation. Not your racing thoughts. Just... texture. Temperature. Pressure. Weight.

Your nervous system can only fully process a limited number of inputs at once. When you consciously redirect your attention to tactile sensation, you're essentially creating a detour for the anxiety. You're not fighting it or trying to make it go away. You're just... diluting its dominance.

Sarah was the first person I tried this with—a software engineer who'd built a successful career on her ability to anticipate problems before they happened. Brilliant at debugging code. Less brilliant at debugging her own nervous system, which ran a constant background process of worry. She'd tried meditation apps. They made her want to throw her phone across the room.

We started smaller. I asked her to notice the feeling of her hands resting on her lap. That's it. No breathing pattern to follow. No visualization to maintain. Just: what do your hands feel like right now?

"Warm," she said after a moment. "And... my left palm is sweating a little. My right hand feels cooler."

"Good. Stay with that for another few seconds."

She did. And something shifted in her face—a slight softening around her eyes.

"That's weird," she said. "I feel... I don't know. Less stuck?"

We built from there. Sarah started carrying a small river stone in her pocket—smooth on one side, rough on the other. During meetings, while reviewing code, even while walking to her car, she'd slip her hand into her pocket and run her thumb across the surface. The smoothness. The roughness. The cool weight of it.

It didn't cure her anxiety. She still worried about edge cases and potential bugs. But it gave her a way to interrupt the spiral before it consumed her. When she felt her thoughts accelerating into catastrophe territory, she didn't try to stop them. She just... noticed them. Then shifted her attention back to the stone.

"It's like having a pause button," she told me weeks later. "Not a stop button. Just... pause. Enough to remember I have a choice about where to put my attention."

The key is that this works with your natural wiring, not against it. You don't have to empty your mind or achieve perfect stillness. You just have to notice something physical. The fabric of your shirt against your skin. The weight of your feet on the floor. The temperature of the air on your face.

Your body is already sending you information. You've just been trained to override it in favor of productivity. Tactile grounding is about briefly reversing that—tuning in instead of tuning out.

Then there's movement. Not exercise—I'm not talking about going for a run or hitting the gym, though those can help too. I mean tiny adjustments. Micro-movements. The kind that no one else would even notice.

Because here's what happens when anxiety lives in your body: it creates pockets of tension that build and build until you're carrying them everywhere. A clenched jaw. Shoulders hiked up near your ears. Fists curled without you realizing it. You've held that tension so long it starts to feel normal. You forget your jaw isn't supposed to ache by 3 PM.

I certainly did. For years, I woke up with headaches and blamed my pillow. My mattress. The weather. Anything but the fact that I'd been grinding my teeth all night, my jaw locked in the same defensive position I held it in during the day.

It took my dentist to point it out. "You're wearing down your molars," she said, showing me X-rays. "Do you clench your jaw?"

I had no idea. I'd been doing it so long I couldn't remember not doing it.

Once I knew to look for it, I started noticing. How my jaw tightened during work calls. While driving. While reading emails. Basically anytime I was awake and vertical. And the more I noticed it, the more I realized I had no idea how to make it stop.

That's where micro-movements came in. Not relaxation—that felt like too much pressure—but tiny, deliberate adjustments. Opening my mouth slightly, moving my jaw side to side. Rolling my shoulders back and down, not to "fix" the tension but just to interrupt the pattern. Uncurling my fists and shaking out my hands for three seconds.

These movements are so small you can do them in the middle of a meeting and no one notices. You're not drawing attention to yourself. You're not stepping out to "take a moment." You're just... adjusting. Releasing a bit of the pressure valve.

Michael—an architect I worked with—described it perfectly. He carried his stress in his shoulders, hiking them up so high he looked like he was perpetually shrugging. Every project was personal to him. Every design decision felt weighted with consequence. By the end of the day, his upper back was a knot of pain.

We introduced shoulder rolls. Tiny ones, the kind you could do while reviewing blueprints or talking to a client. Just a gentle rotation backward, then forward. Combined with deliberately dropping his shoulders down away from his ears—something he had to consciously remember to do because his default position had them practically touching.

“It feels stupid at first,” he admitted. “Like, how is this supposed to help? But then you do it a few times and you realize... oh. I’ve been holding my shoulders up like this for hours. Of course my back hurts.”

The point isn’t that micro-movements fix anxiety. They don’t. But they give you a way to work with the physical manifestation of it. They remind your nervous system that you’re not actually in danger, even though it feels like you are. That you have agency over your body, even when your thoughts are spinning.

And sometimes, that physical shift is enough to create a little breathing room for everything else.

But here’s where it gets more challenging. Because tactile grounding and micro-movements address the physical symptoms—the tension, the racing heart, the shallow breathing. They help you manage the body’s response. But what about the mental component? The thoughts?

This is where people with high-functioning anxiety often get stuck. Because the thoughts don’t feel irrational. They feel productive. Important. Like if you just think about this problem enough, from enough angles, you’ll finally figure out how to prevent disaster.

Except you never do. The thinking just generates more thinking. More scenarios to prepare for. More potential catastrophes to prevent.

I used to lie awake running through conversations I needed to have the next day, scripting out every possible response and counter-response. I told myself I was being prepared. Responsible. That this was just what you did when you took things seriously.

What I was actually doing was exhausting myself trying to control outcomes I had no power over.

The shift came when I started treating these thoughts differently. Not as problems to solve, but as... data. Information my brain was offering me, which I could acknowledge without necessarily acting on.

This is interoceptive exposure—but applied to thoughts, not just sensations. It's the practice of noticing what your mind is doing without immediately trying to fix it or shut it down. Of sitting with the discomfort of not knowing how a conversation will go, or whether you'll meet a deadline, or if that email came across wrong.

It sounds passive. It's not. It's actually one of the hardest things I've ever learned to do.

Because every instinct in you wants to engage with the anxious thought. To pick it apart, examine it, prepare for it. Your anxiety has convinced you that thinking about it more will make you safer. And maybe sometimes it does. Maybe sometimes that preparation pays off.

But most of the time? You're just strengthening the pathway. Teaching your brain that anxious thoughts require immediate attention and response.

Interoceptive exposure asks you to do the opposite. To notice the thought—"What if I mess up this presentation?"—and instead of spiraling into planning mode, just... observe it. Feel the sensation that comes with it. The tightness in your chest. The flutter in your stomach. The urge to grab your phone and recheck your notes for the fifteenth time.

And then, instead of acting on that urge, you sit with it. Just for a moment.

Not forever. I'm not suggesting you ignore legitimate preparation needs. But just long enough to prove to your nervous system that the urge to immediately respond isn't a command. It's just... an urge. It doesn't control you.

Rachel, a lawyer I worked with, found this almost unbearable at first. Her entire career was built on preparation. On anticipating every argument the opposing counsel might make. On being three steps ahead at all times. The idea of not following through on an anxious thought felt reckless. Dangerous.

We started with small stakes. Not case preparation—that felt too loaded. But everyday worries. "What if I'm late to this meeting?" Instead of immediately checking her calendar, calculating drive time, and leaving twenty minutes early, she practiced sitting with the thought for sixty seconds. Noticing the urge to check. The discomfort of not checking. The sensation of uncertainty in her body.

"It feels like I'm going to forget something important," she said.

"I know. But you're not. You're just not checking right this second."

After sixty seconds, she could check. And usually, she did. But that minute of sitting with the discomfort started to stretch. Sometimes she could wait two minutes. Then five. Not because she was trying to prove something, but because she was learning—in her body, not just her head—that the urgency she felt wasn't always accurate.

The anxious thought said: This is an emergency. You need to act now.

But her body, when she actually listened to it, said: This is uncomfortable. But you're okay.

Over time, Rachel got better at distinguishing between thoughts that required action and thoughts that just required acknowledgment. Her anxiety didn't disappear. But it stopped running the show.

The truth is, none of these tools eliminate anxiety. They're not designed to. And I think that's actually why they work for people like us—people who've spent years being told we just need to relax, just need to calm down, just need to not be so intense.

We don't need to become different people. We need to work with who we already are.

Tactile grounding doesn't make you less driven. It gives you a way to manage the intensity without being consumed by it. Micro-movements don't erase your perfectionism. They prevent your body from paying the price for it. Interoceptive exposure doesn't silence the worried thoughts. It changes your relationship to them.

These are tools for staying functional—genuinely functional, not just white-knuckling your way through. Tools that fit into the margins of your day. That don't require you to carve out time you don't have or become someone you're not.

But here's what I want you to sit with, the question I wish someone had asked me years ago:

What if the anxiety you're managing so skillfully isn't actually serving you anymore? What if the vigilance that once protected you is now just... exhausting you? What if being "high-functioning" has become another way of saying you've gotten really good at pushing through, at the cost of actually living?

Because there's a difference between resilience and resignation. Between adaptation and acceptance. And sometimes the most functional thing you can do is stop asking how to manage the anxiety better, and start asking why you're carrying so much of it in the first place.

That's the territory we're heading into next. Not how to cope with the performance trap—but how it got built, and whether you still want to live inside it.

The tools you've probably tried—deep breathing, progressive muscle relaxation, guided meditation apps that tell you to "just be present"—aren't wrong, exactly. They're just designed for a different kind of nervous system. They're built for people who need help slowing down because they've ground to a halt. But you? You're not stuck in neutral. You're redlining in fifth gear, and someone telling you to "take three deep breaths" feels about as useful as handing you a bicycle helmet during a car crash.

What you need aren't tools that slow you down. You need tools that meet you where you are—moving, thinking, doing—and work *with* your momentum instead of against it.

So let's start there. With regulation strategies that don't require you to stop being who you are.

Bilateral stimulation is one of the quietest, most underrated tools in the anxiety toolkit, probably because it sounds too simple to work. The premise: alternating left-right input to your body—tapping your knees, walking, even chewing gum—activates both hemispheres of your brain in a way that helps process emotional intensity without requiring you to sit still and *feel your feelings*.

It's the neurological equivalent of shaking out a tangled cord. You're not stopping the signal. You're just giving it somewhere to move.

For high-functioning anxiety, this is gold. You can do it while you work. While you walk. While you're on a call. Tap your fingers on the desk, alternating left and right. Shift your weight from foot to foot while you're standing at the counter. Even eye movements—looking left, then right, in a slow rhythm—can help. It doesn't look like self-care. It doesn't feel performative. It just quietly pulls some of the charge out of your system while you keep going.

The research on this comes largely from EMDR (Eye Movement Desensitization and Reprocessing), a trauma therapy that uses bilateral stimulation to help the brain process distressing memories. But you don't need to be working through trauma for this to be useful. Anxiety, at its core, is your nervous system stuck in a loop—and bilateral input helps interrupt that loop without demanding you stop everything and meditate.

Micro-dosing stillness is another one. Because here's the thing: if you're someone whose anxiety spikes the moment you try to "relax," forcing yourself into a 20-minute meditation is just going to reinforce the idea that stillness is dangerous. Your nervous system will treat it like a threat, not a remedy.

So instead of trying to meditate for longer than your system can tolerate, try for less. Radically less. Ten seconds. Literally. Close your eyes, take one full breath, and open them again. That's it. No app. No guided voice. No expectation that you're going to Feel Peaceful or Achieve Presence. Just ten seconds of pause.

Do that three times a day, and you've given your nervous system 30 seconds of practice with the idea that stopping doesn't mean collapsing. That stillness doesn't have to mean vulnerability. Over time, your tolerance builds—not because you're forcing it, but because you're training your body to recognize that nothing bad happens when you pause.

This is the opposite of the "just meditate more" advice that probably already makes you feel like a failure. This is about meeting your nervous system where it actually is, and building capacity incrementally, the same way you'd build strength in a muscle that's been injured.

Containment strategies are the unsung heroes of high-functioning anxiety regulation. Because sometimes the problem isn't that you're feeling too much—it's that you're feeling it all at once, in the middle of a meeting or a project or a conversation, and you don't have the luxury of falling apart right now.

So you need a way to say, "Not now. Later."

This isn't suppression. Suppression is pretending the feeling doesn't exist. Containment is acknowledging it exists, and choosing when you're going to deal with it. It's the difference between shoving something in a closet and hoping it disappears, and putting something in a labeled box that you'll open at 7 p.m.

Here's how it works in practice: when the wave of anxiety hits—say, halfway through your inbox, or in the middle of a work presentation—you don't try to make it go away. You don't tell yourself it's not a big deal. You just mentally label it: "This is the fear that I'm not doing enough. I see it. I'll come back to it tonight."

And then, critically, you actually do. You set a timer for 15 minutes that evening, sit down, and let yourself feel it. Write about it. Cry if you need to. Let it be as big as it wants to be, in a space where it's safe to do so.

The reason this works is because your nervous system isn't stupid. It knows when you're lying to it. If you say "I'll deal with this later" and then never do, it stops trusting you. It'll escalate. It'll interrupt you at worse and worse times, because it's learned that's the only way to get your attention.

But if you follow through—if you actually make space for the feeling later—your system learns that "later" is real. And the next time you say "not now," it's more likely to believe you.

Somatic grounding gets thrown around a lot in therapy-speak, but most explanations make it sound more complicated than it is. At its core, it's just this: noticing what your body is doing right now, in this moment, without trying to change it.

Not "relax your shoulders." Not "unclench your jaw." Just: "My shoulders are up by my ears. My jaw is tight. My hands are cold."

The act of noticing, without judgment or correction, does something really specific: it moves you out of the future (where anxiety lives) and into the present (where your body actually is). It's not about fixing anything. It's about interrupting the spiral.

And for high-functioning anxiety, this is critical, because so much of your distress is about what *might* happen, what you *should* be doing, what you *haven't* done yet. Your mind is three steps ahead, cataloging risks and scanning for problems. But your body? Your body is just here. Sitting in this chair. Breathing this breath.

When you ground yourself somatically, you're not trying to calm down. You're just re-establishing contact with the present. And sometimes that's enough to take the edge off.

Try this: right now, without moving, notice five things your body is touching. The chair under you. Your feet on the floor. Your shirt against your skin. The phone or book in your hand. The air on your face.

That's it. You don't have to do anything with that information. You're just collecting data. And in doing so, you're pulling yourself out of the anxiety spiral and back into the room.

Energy matching is a concept borrowed from polyvagal theory, and it's one of the most validating tools I've encountered for high-functioning anxiety. The idea is simple: you don't have to calm down to regulate. You can regulate *up*.

Most anxiety advice assumes the goal is to get calmer, quieter, slower. But what if your system is revving because it *needs* to move energy through? What if the jittery, restless, can't-sit-still feeling isn't a problem to be solved—it's a signal that your body needs to discharge something?

In that case, trying to force yourself into calm is just going to create more tension. What you need is movement that matches the intensity of what you're feeling. Not a gentle yoga flow. Not a slow walk. Something that meets your nervous system at its current speed.

Go for a hard run. Do jumping jacks in your kitchen. Shake your whole body for 60 seconds like you're trying to fling water off your hands. Scream into a pillow. Rip up paper. Pound your fists into a couch cushion.

It sounds chaotic. It is chaotic. But chaos isn't the same as dysregulation. Sometimes chaos is exactly what regulation looks like when you've been holding everything together too tightly for too long.

The point isn't to "get it all out" in some cathartic release. The point is to give your body permission to express the intensity it's holding, so it doesn't have to keep holding it as tension.

And here's the thing: once you've moved that energy through, *then* you can access calm. But trying to get there without first honoring the intensity is like trying to whisper when you need to yell. It just doesn't work.

Micro-choices are another underrated tool. High-functioning anxiety often comes with a paralyzing sense that everything matters too much, that every decision carries weight, that you can't afford to get anything wrong. So you end up frozen, or spinning, or second-guessing every move.

One way to interrupt that is to practice making decisions that *don't* matter. Tiny, inconsequential choices that you make quickly, without deliberation, just to remind your nervous system that not everything is life-or-death.

What mug do you use for your coffee? Pick one in three seconds. Which route do you take to the grocery store? Choose without weighing the options. What do you eat for lunch? First thing that sounds good.

This isn't about being reckless. It's about recalibrating your threat-detection system. Because when you treat every choice like it's critical, your brain stays in high alert. But when you practice making low-stakes decisions quickly, you start to rebuild trust in your own judgment. You start to remember that most things are reversible. That most mistakes are survivable. That not everything requires a cost-benefit analysis.

And over time, that ease starts to bleed into the bigger decisions too.

Externalizing the inner critic is a cognitive tool that works specifically well for the kind of anxiety that shows up as relentless self-monitoring. You know the voice. The one that's always scanning for what you did wrong, what you should have said differently, what you're about to mess up.

Most advice tells you to challenge that voice. To reframe it. To replace it with something kinder.

But what if, instead of arguing with it, you just... stepped back from it?

Here's the practice: the next time that critical voice pipes up, imagine it as a separate character. Give it a face, a name, a tone. Not to mock it, but to create distance. Some people imagine it as an anxious news anchor, catastrophizing every minor event. Others see it as an overcaffeinated life coach who's never satisfied. Some people just picture it as a parrot on their shoulder, repeating the same five phrases over and over.

The goal isn't to make it go away. The goal is to stop identifying with it. To recognize that the voice is *in* you, but it's not *you*.

Once you've externalized it, you can respond to it differently. Instead of believing it or fighting it, you can just... acknowledge it. "Okay, there's the catastrophizing again. Got it." And then you can choose whether to engage with it or not.

This is a subtle shift, but it's powerful. Because as long as you believe that anxious voice *is* you, you have to take it seriously. But once you recognize it's just one part of a larger system—a part that's trying to protect you, sure, but not the whole truth—you get your agency back.

Pre-deciding is a tool for decision fatigue, which is a massive but often invisible driver of high-functioning anxiety. When you're constantly in motion, constantly optimizing, constantly making a hundred small choices a day, your cognitive load becomes unsustainable. And that's when everything starts to feel hard.

So instead of deciding in the moment, you decide in advance.

You pre-decide what you're eating for breakfast. What you're wearing on Tuesday. What time you're going to bed. What your answer is when someone asks you to take on a new project.

This isn't about rigidity. It's about reducing the number of decisions you have to make when you're already running on fumes. Because when you're anxious, even small decisions feel enormous. And if you can take a few of those off the table, you free up bandwidth for the things that actually matter.

Some people pre-decide their boundaries. "I don't work past 7 p.m." "I don't check email on weekends." "I say no to any commitment that doesn't excite me or serve a clear goal."

Some people pre-decide their routines. Morning, evening, how they transition between work and home.

The specifics don't matter. What matters is that you're not reinventing the wheel every single day. You're creating a structure that holds you, so you don't have to hold everything yourself.

These tools—bilateral stimulation, micro-stillness, containment, somatic grounding, energy matching, micro-choices, externalizing the critic, pre-deciding—aren't a cure. They're not going to make the anxiety disappear. But they also don't require you to stop, to slow down, to become someone you're not.

They work *with* the momentum. With the intensity. With the reality that you're not going to suddenly become a person who meditates for an hour every morning or finds peace in doing less.

What they offer instead is something more sustainable: a way to stay in motion without burning out. A way to regulate without shutting down. A way to be high-functioning without it costing you everything.

Because the goal isn't to stop being capable. It's to stop mistaking capacity for invincibility. To recognize that you can be good at what you do *and* need support. That you can be driven *and* need rest. That being functional doesn't mean you have to function alone.

Chapter 4: The Performance Trap

In 2018, Simone Biles walked away from the vault final at the Tokyo Olympics. Not because she was injured—at least not in the way we typically understand injury. She'd lost what gymnasts call "the twisties," a disorienting condition where your body and brain disconnect mid-air. You know what trick you're supposed to do. You've done it ten thousand times. But suddenly, in the moment that matters most, you can't find yourself in space.

The internet exploded. Half of it rallied around her courage. The other half called her a quitter.

Here's what I kept thinking about, though: the twenty years before that moment. The training sessions where a slight wobble on a dismount meant staying late to run it again. And again. The competitions where anything less than gold felt like failure. The internalized message that your value—to your team, your country, yourself—hinged on executing perfectly under pressure.

Biles didn't lose her nerve that day. She'd been running on it for two decades.

That's the performance trap. Not the single moment when the system finally crashes. It's all the moments before—the ones where we override what our bodies are trying to tell us because we've trained ourselves to believe that anything less than flawless execution is unacceptable.

I prepared for a client presentation by rehearsing it 47 times. Slept three hours. Delivered it "perfectly" according to the feedback. Then sat in my car in the parking garage for twenty minutes afterward, unable to remember if I'd locked my front door that morning. That moment—my nervous system finally getting my attention after weeks of override—is when I realized the cost of what I'd been calling "high standards."

The thing is, I drove home that day and the door was fine. Locked or unlocked, it didn't matter—nothing had happened. But I couldn't remember the last morning I'd left the house without that gnawing should-I-go-back-and-check feeling. Couldn't remember the last presentation I'd walked away from feeling satisfied instead of already scanning for what I could have done better. The performance had been perfect. I'd been disintegrating.

Dr. Amelia Hayes is the kind of cardiologist other doctors send their own parents to. Meticulous. Brilliant. The type who stays late reviewing charts, who triple-checks medication interactions, who's known for catching the subtle things other physicians miss.

She's also the type who, on a Tuesday morning, stands in the hospital corridor holding an ECG printout, staring at it for the fourth time in twenty minutes.

The patient is stable. The arrhythmia is complex but manageable. The treatment plan is sound—she knows it's sound, she's been doing this for fifteen years. But what if she's missing something? What if there's a drug interaction she hasn't considered? What if this particular patient has some underlying condition that makes the standard protocol risky?

Her hands are steady as she holds the printout. That's the thing—from the outside, she looks completely composed. Confident, even. Inside, her heart rate is climbing. Her jaw is clenched. There's a tightness spreading across her chest that has nothing to do with cardiac pathology and everything to do with the impossibility of what she's demanding from herself.

Perfection.

Not excellence. Not "doing her best." Perfection. The kind where a single overlooked detail could—in her mind—lead to catastrophe. Where "good enough" doesn't exist as a category.

This isn't about Amelia being bad at her job. She's exceptional at it. This is about what happens when your nervous system can't tell the difference between "I need to be careful" and "I need to be perfect." When the physiological response to pressure—the cortisol, the adrenaline, the heightened vigilance—stops being a helpful acute response and becomes your baseline.

Your body is trying to protect you. It just doesn't realize it's the one you need protection from.

The morning I met Amelia, she was forty minutes into our first session before she mentioned the panic attack she'd had in the physician's lounge three weeks earlier. Just slipped it in, casual, like she was mentioning she'd had toast for breakfast. "It was fine," she said. "I just needed a minute."

I asked what had triggered it.

She'd been reviewing a discharge summary. Routine case. Uncomplicated. But she'd noticed—or thought she'd noticed—a potential issue with the medication dosing. Probably nothing. Almost certainly nothing. But she couldn't let it go. She'd pulled the patient's full chart, cross-referenced every medication, recalculated the dosing three different ways. Everything checked out. She knew everything checked out.

Her body didn't care. Heart pounding, vision narrowing, hands shaking so hard she had to set down her coffee.

"It passed," she said. "I just breathed through it."

Like this was a normal Tuesday. Like having a panic attack over a routine chart review was just part of the job.

Here's what was happening in Amelia's body while she stood in that corridor, and later in the lounge, and probably a dozen other times she didn't mention:

Her amygdala—the part of the brain that acts as a threat detector—had flagged these situations as dangerous. Not "patient in cardiac arrest" dangerous. "You might make a mistake" dangerous. To her amygdala, trained by years of holding herself to impossible standards, those two threats registered the same.

So it did what it's designed to do: it triggered the sympathetic nervous system. Cortisol flooded her bloodstream. Her heart rate increased. Blood flow was redirected from her digestive system to her large muscle groups, preparing her to fight or flee. Her pupils dilated slightly. Her hearing sharpened.

None of this is conscious. None of it is a choice.

And none of it is helpful for what she actually needs to do, which is think clearly about a complex medical case.

But here's the cruel part: this response *feels* necessary. The anxiety tells her that this hypervigilance is what's keeping her patients safe. That if she relaxes—if she trusts her training and makes a decision without quintuple-checking everything—something terrible will happen.

So she checks again.

And the relief lasts maybe thirty seconds before the doubt creeps back in.

This is the performance trap's signature move: it convinces you that the anxiety is functional. That it's what makes you good at what you do. That other people might be able to relax their standards, but you—you can't afford to. Not in your field. Not with these stakes.

I used to think the same thing. I'd tell myself that my tendency to over-prepare wasn't anxiety, it was professionalism. That my habit of running through every possible failure scenario wasn't catastrophizing, it was thorough planning. That the physical tension I carried through every high-stakes situation wasn't a problem—it was just what focus felt like.

Then I started noticing what happened *after* those situations. The crash. The exhaustion. The inability to feel satisfaction even when things went well, because I was already scanning ahead to the next potential failure.

That's when I realized: this wasn't high-functioning anxiety. It was just anxiety that had learned to disguise itself as competence.

And the disguise was so good I'd been defending it for years.

The thing about perfectionism is that it doesn't announce itself as a problem. It shows up wearing the costume of excellence. Of high standards. Of caring about your work.

Marcus—a partner at a major law firm, brilliant legal mind, known for catching details other attorneys missed—came to see me because he was convinced he was developing early-onset Parkinson's. The tremor in his hands during oral arguments was getting worse.

We ran through his typical week. The late nights. The obsessive brief reviews. The pre-argument ritual where he'd run through every possible question the judge might ask, then every possible follow-up to his answers, then contingency responses to those.

Also: the emails sent at 2 AM. The briefs reviewed so many times he could recite them verbatim. The tremor that no one but him seemed to notice.

"How do you feel right before you walk into court?" I asked.

"Focused," he said immediately.

I waited.

"...and kind of sick," he added. "Heart racing. Hands shaking. But that's just adrenaline. That's normal before a big argument."

"Is it normal the night before? Two nights before?"

He paused. "I thought that meant I cared about doing a good job."

Here's what Marcus's body was trying to tell him: *This isn't sustainable. You're asking me to maintain emergency-level activation for days at a time. I'm not designed for that.*

The tremor wasn't neurological. It was his nervous system's distress signal, cranked up so loud he finally couldn't ignore it.

But even then—even sitting in my office, talking about the physical toll this was taking—part of him was still convinced the problem was that he wasn't managing the anxiety well enough. That other attorneys must have some secret for maintaining this pace without falling apart, and if he could just figure out what it was, he could keep going.

That's how deep the performance trap runs. It reframes your body's distress signals as personal failures. As evidence that you're not tough enough, disciplined enough, committed enough.

When really, your body is the only thing in this equation that's telling you the truth.

The cognitive patterns underlying the performance trap are surprisingly consistent across people and professions, though they show up in different disguises.

All-or-nothing thinking is usually the foundation. You know this one intimately if you've ever spent three hours on a project that's 95% done, agonizing over the last 5% because "good enough" feels like failure.

Sarah—a project manager I worked with—once spent an entire evening reformatting a presentation deck because the alignment of text boxes was "off by a few pixels." The content was solid. The data was compelling. The recommendations were clear.

But the text boxes.

When I asked what she thought would happen if she left them slightly misaligned, she said, "People will think I don't care about details."

"Will they?"

"...probably not. But I'll know."

And there it is. All-or-nothing thinking isn't usually about what others will think. It's about an internal standard that has no room for "mostly good" or "perfectly adequate for the context."

It's binary. Perfect or worthless. And since perfection is impossible, you're left in a perpetual state of falling short.

The exhausting part isn't even the extra hours spent on the text boxes or the brief review or the presentation rehearsal. It's the constant low-grade sense of inadequacy. The way nothing you do ever quite measures up. The way completion doesn't bring satisfaction, just temporary relief before the next thing.

I had a client—software developer, smart guy—who told me he couldn't enjoy the product launch party his team threw because all he could think about was a feature he'd wanted to include but hadn't had time to build. The product was successful. Users loved it. His team was celebrating.

He was cataloging everything that wasn't there.

Then there's catastrophic prediction, which is where things get really creative.

You're not just worried about making a mistake. You're constructing elaborate disaster scenarios where a single error cascades into career-ending, relationship-destroying, identity-shattering catastrophe.

David, a software engineer, once told me he stayed up until 4 AM fixing a bug in code that wasn't going live for another week. When I asked what he thought would happen if the bug made it to production, he said, "The app could crash. Users would be frustrated. The team would lose confidence in me. I'd probably get put on a performance improvement plan. Eventually I'd get fired. I'd have trouble finding another job because of the gap in my resume. I'd end up—"

I stopped him. "How many steps are we from the original bug?"

He counted. "Seven."

"And how many of those steps are things that have actually happened before?"

"...none of them."

Your brain doesn't care. When you're in the grip of catastrophic thinking, each step feels inevitable. The anxiety isn't responding to the actual risk—it's responding to the imagined catastrophe. And because the catastrophe feels so real, the anxiety feels justified. Necessary, even.

Here's what I've noticed, though, both in my own experience and working with clients: the catastrophic predictions almost never come true. But they don't have to. They do their damage just by existing.

Because once your brain has constructed the seven-step path from minor bug to unemployment, you can't un-see it. It's there in the background every time you write code, every time you submit work, every time you make a decision that carries any possibility of error.

Which is every decision.

So you find yourself trying to prevent disasters that exist only in your imagination. Spending real time, real energy, real life trying to outrun ghosts.

And then there's the need for external validation, which is maybe the most exhausting pattern of all.

When your internal sense of worth is unstable, you start outsourcing it. You need others to confirm that you're competent, valuable, doing it right.

This one's particularly brutal because external validation is inherently unreliable. People don't always respond immediately to your emails. Managers don't always give effusive praise. Clients sometimes have neutral reactions to excellent work.

And when you're dependent on that external confirmation, every ambiguous response feels like rejection.

Elena, a graphic designer, would refresh her email obsessively after sending work to clients. If she didn't get a response within a few hours, she'd start spiraling: *They hate it. They're trying to figure out how to tell me it's terrible. They're looking for another designer.*

The irony? Her work was consistently excellent. Clients loved working with her. But she couldn't internalize that. Each project started from zero, requiring fresh proof of her competence.

I asked her once what it would take for her to feel confident in her skills.

She thought about it for a long time. “I don’t know,” she finally said. “I guess... if clients always responded immediately? And always loved everything? But that’s not realistic.”

“Right. So you’ve set up a system where confidence is impossible.”

She looked startled. Then sad. “I guess I have.”

The need for external validation keeps you trapped in a loop where your sense of worth is always conditional, always precarious, always just one ambiguous email away from collapse. And the worst part is, the more you seek that validation, the more hollow it feels when you get it.

Because deep down, you know: if you need someone else to tell you you’re doing okay, their reassurance can’t actually fix the doubt. It just quiets it temporarily.

These patterns don’t operate in isolation. They feed each other, creating what I think of as a closed anxiety loop.

All-or-nothing thinking means any small imperfection triggers catastrophic predictions. Catastrophic predictions heighten your need for external validation to reassure you that disaster isn’t imminent. And when that validation is delayed or ambiguous, it confirms your worst fears, reinforcing the all-or-nothing framework.

It’s self-sustaining. And like Amelia standing in that hospital corridor, the more you try to think your way out, the tighter it gets.

Because you can't think your way out of a nervous system problem.

You can't logic yourself into feeling safe when your body is screaming danger. You can't convince your amygdala that the stakes aren't actually that high, not when it's already flooded you with cortisol and adrenaline and locked you into threat-response mode.

What you *can* do is interrupt the loop. Introduce something that doesn't fit the pattern. Give your nervous system evidence that contradicts its predictions.

This is where controlled imperfection becomes not just helpful but essential.

We started with Amelia and her single chart review. Just once, instead of three or four times. Put it down and do something else.

She looked at me like I'd suggested she show up to surgery drunk.

"What if they ask about something I don't remember?" she said.

"Then you'll say, 'Let me pull up your chart to make sure I give you accurate information,' and you'll look it up right then."

"But that makes me look unprepared."

"Does it? Or does it make you look like someone who double-checks information before giving medical advice?"

We went back and forth. Eventually, she agreed to try it. Low-stakes patient, routine follow-up, straightforward case.

The day of the appointment, she texted me: *This is excruciating.*

Then, an hour later: *Patient didn't notice anything different. I feel like I ran a marathon.*

That physical exhaustion? That was her nervous system recalibrating. For years, it had been operating on the belief that multiple chart reviews equaled safety. Now it had evidence—direct, embodied evidence—that she could function effectively with less preparation.

Did it feel natural immediately? No.

Did it eliminate her anxiety overnight? Absolutely not.

But it created a crack in the belief system. A small piece of proof that maybe, just maybe, perfection wasn't actually the price of safety.

And here's what happened over the next few weeks: Amelia kept doing it. Single chart review. Then the appointment. Sometimes patients asked questions she hadn't anticipated. Sometimes she had to look things up in the moment.

And every time—every single time—the disaster she feared didn't happen.

The gap between what her anxiety predicted and what actually occurred started to widen. And in that gap, something shifted.

Not her competence. That was never the problem. Her nervous system's calibration of what "safe" looked like.

You're probably thinking: okay, but that's a low-stakes situation. What about when it actually matters?

Fair question. And here's the thing—the performance trap is particularly insidious in high-stakes fields precisely because the fear isn't completely irrational. Mistakes in medicine, in law, in engineering, in any number of professions *can* have serious consequences.

But here's what we tend to miss: anxiety-driven perfectionism doesn't actually make you better at preventing those mistakes.

In fact, it often makes you worse.

When you're operating from a place of chronic hypervigilance, your brain is flooded with stress hormones that impair executive function. Your working memory gets compromised. Your ability to think flexibly—to adapt when unexpected situations arise—deteriorates. You become rigid, formulaic.

You're not operating at your best. You're operating in survival mode.

And you're so focused on avoiding mistakes that you can't see the one you're actively making: burning yourself to the ground in the name of standards you'd never apply to anyone else.

I see this play out over and over. The lawyer who's so anxious about missing a detail in a brief that they review it twelve times and, in their exhaustion, actually *introduce* errors in the final version. The project manager whose team starts making decisions without consulting them because they know the response will be "let me think about it more" followed by three days of analysis paralysis. The designer who's so focused on pixel-perfect alignment that they miss the deadline entirely.

The perfectionism isn't preventing failure. It's creating it.

And your body knows. That's why it's sending those distress signals—the tremor, the panic attacks, the chest tightness, the inability to sleep. It's trying to tell you: this strategy isn't working.

There's another piece of this that's easy to miss: the role of identity.

For many people caught in the performance trap, perfectionism isn't just a behavior—it's who they think they are.

"I'm the person who gets things right."

"I'm the one people can count on."

"I'm detail-oriented."

These aren't inherently bad self-concepts. The problem is when they become so rigid that any deviation feels like an identity crisis.

Jordan was a high school teacher known for her meticulously organized lesson plans and thoughtfully crafted feedback on student work. She spent hours each week writing detailed comments on essays, customizing feedback for each student's learning style.

It was meaningful work. Her students appreciated it. But it was also unsustainable.

By November of each school year, she was exhausted. Resentful. Crying in her car before going into the building. And then feeling guilty about the resentment, because wasn't this what good teachers did?

When I suggested she might scale back the written feedback—maybe detailed comments on major assignments, more streamlined feedback on smaller ones—she looked stricken.

"But that's what makes me a good teacher," she said.

"Is it? Or is thoughtful feedback what makes you a good teacher, and you've decided thoughtful has to mean exhaustive?"

She sat with that for a while.

"If I give less detailed feedback, I'm not living up to my own standards."

"Whose standards are those, really?"

Another long pause.

"I don't know anymore."

This is the performance trap's deepest hook: it convinces you that the unsustainable thing you're doing is essential to who you are. That if you stop doing it, you won't just be choosing differently—you'll be betraying yourself.

The identity piece is why "just relax your standards" doesn't work as advice. You're not asking someone to do less work. You're asking them to become a different person. Or at least, that's how it feels.

Here's what Jordan eventually discovered: she didn't become a worse teacher when she streamlined her feedback process. She became a more sustainable one.

And ironically, because she wasn't so depleted, she was more present in the classroom. More creative in her lesson planning. More emotionally available to students who needed support.

The thing she thought defined her excellence was actually limiting it.

But that realization didn't come from me telling her it would be fine. It came from her trying it—reluctantly, anxiously—and discovering through direct experience that the catastrophe she feared didn't materialize.

Her students didn't revolt. Her principal didn't reprimand her. She didn't lose her sense of identity as a good teacher.

What she did lose: the resentment. The Sunday-night dread. The crying in the car.

Small trade-off.

Let's get practical, because knowing all this intellectually doesn't change much if you don't do anything different.

If you're reading this and recognizing yourself in these patterns, here's where to start.

Pick something small. Something that triggers your perfectionism but has low actual stakes.

Maybe it's sending an email with a minor typo you noticed after hitting send. Don't send a correction. Don't apologize in a follow-up. Just... let it exist.

Maybe it's submitting a report that's thorough and complete but not quite as polished as you'd normally make it. Hit submit before you do the fifth editing pass.

Maybe it's showing up to a meeting having reviewed the materials once instead of three times.

The specifics matter less than the principle: you're deliberately choosing "good enough" in a situation where your anxiety insists on perfect.

Then—and this is crucial—you pay attention to what happens.

Not just externally (though you'll probably notice that the catastrophe you feared doesn't materialize).

But internally. Notice what your body does. Notice the surge of anxiety, the urge to fix or correct or over-explain.

And then notice what happens after.

The anxiety peaks. It doesn't feel good. Your heart might race. Your stomach might clench. Every part of you will be screaming to go back and fix it, to make it right, to bring it up to your standards.

Don't.

Sit with the discomfort. Let it be there without trying to make it go away.

And here's what you'll discover: it peaks, and then—if you don't feed it by engaging in your usual perfectionistic behaviors—it starts to come down.

That descent, that return to baseline, is evidence. Your nervous system is learning: discomfort isn't danger. Imperfection isn't catastrophe.

The email with the typo doesn't torpedo your career. The slightly-less-polished report gets read and understood just fine. The meeting you were moderately prepared for instead of exhaustively prepared for goes smoothly.

And each time this happens, you're building a new data set. A new reference library for your nervous system to draw from when it's trying to determine how much threat-response is warranted.

Do it again. And again. Gradually increasing the stakes as your tolerance builds.

This isn't about becoming careless. It's about recalibrating what "careful enough" means. It's about building trust—in yourself, in your skills, in your ability to handle imperfection without it defining you.

I worked with a software developer who started by allowing himself to submit code for review after testing it thoroughly but not exhaustively. His usual pattern was to run every possible edge case he could imagine, which could take hours.

The new pattern: test the main functionality and the most likely edge cases. Submit.

First few times, he had to physically close his laptop and leave the room to stop himself from running just one more test.

But here's what happened: sometimes his colleagues found bugs in code review. And instead of this being the career-ending disaster his anxiety predicted, it was... normal. Expected, even. That's what code review is for.

And sometimes—most of the time, actually—his code was fine. The extra two hours of edge-case testing he used to do weren't actually preventing problems. They were just feeding his anxiety.

After a few months of this, he told me something that stuck with me: "I thought if I wasn't anxious, I wouldn't be careful. But I'm actually catching more bugs now, because I'm not so exhausted that I'm sloppy."

The anxiety wasn't making him better. It was just making him tired.

One more thing about the performance trap, and it's the piece that took me longest to see in my own life.

The relentless striving isn't just about achieving something external. It's about not having to face something internal.

As long as you're focused on the next deadline, the next performance, the next chance to prove yourself, you don't have to sit with the question underneath it all:

What if I'm already enough?

Not after the next achievement. Not once you've proven yourself one more time. Now. As you are.

That question is terrifying if you've built your entire sense of worth on performance. Because if you're already enough, then what was all that striving for?

And if you stop—if you step off the treadmill of constant proving—what's left?

This is the real reason the performance trap is so hard to escape. It's not just about changing behaviors or managing anxiety. It's about confronting the belief system underneath: the one that says your value is conditional. That you have to earn the right to exist, to take up space, to be treated with kindness.

Including by yourself.

I can't tell you that realization is comfortable. I can't tell you it happens quickly, or that once you see it you're free.

What I can tell you is that the question—*What if I'm already enough?*—is worth sitting with. Even if it makes your anxiety spike. Even if every part of you wants to jump up and find something productive to do to avoid feeling it.

Sit with it anyway.

Because on the other side of that question isn't laziness or mediocrity or the collapse of everything you've built.

It's the thing your body has been trying to tell you all along: you don't have to run this hard to be safe. You never did.

Chapter 5: Boundaries Without Saying 'No'

What happens when you simply *can't* add one more thing to your plate?

Sarah—a graphic designer I worked with maybe six years ago, though it feels like yesterday—called me on a Thursday afternoon. Not scheduled. Just called. And when I picked up, she didn't say hello, didn't apologize for interrupting. She said: "I'm holding oranges."

I waited.

"I mean, I'm *seeing* oranges. In my head. Every time someone asks me to do something, I picture myself holding this growing stack of oranges. One on top of another. And right now someone just asked if I could redesign the entire website navigation by Monday and I swear to God I can feel my hands shaking because I'm trying to balance seventeen oranges and if I add this one—" She stopped. Took a breath that sounded like it hurt. "If I add this one, they all fall."

She wasn't being poetic. She was describing the actual image her brain constructed every time a new request landed. Each orange represented a commitment, and she'd been stacking them all week. Emails. Client revisions. Her daughter's science project. Agreeing to review her colleague's portfolio. Promising her mother she'd come to dinner Sunday. One orange, another, another. And now this.

The thing that struck me—the thing that still strikes me when I think about that call—wasn't the oranges themselves. It was that she called because she genuinely didn't know whether she was allowed to say no. Not *how* to say it. Whether the option even existed.

That's where high-functioning anxiety lives. Not in dramatic breakdowns or obvious distress, but in the quiet, terrible certainty that you have no choice but to say yes. Even when your hands are full. Even when you can feel the physical structure of your life becoming unsound.

I should probably admit something here: I've done the orange thing too. Not oranges, exactly. Books. Stacked spines in my mind, wobbling higher every time I agreed to one more workshop, one more revision, one more "quick call." For years I told myself this was just being responsible, being professional. It took a minor vertigo episode during a keynote—nothing dramatic, just a moment where the room tilted and I gripped the podium—to realize I'd been running the same pattern Sarah had. Ignoring every early signal my body sent until it delivered one I couldn't dismiss.

We do this. Those of us wired toward high-functioning anxiety become shockingly good at overriding our internal warning systems. That tightness in your chest when someone asks for help? You've learned to breathe through it. The way your shoulders creep toward your ears during a meeting where you know you'll be asked to take on another project? Baseline tension. You don't even notice anymore. The quickening pulse, the slight nausea, the sense of *too much*—all of it gets filed under "just being busy" and dismissed.

But your body is keeping score.

Think back—and I mean really reach back—to your earliest memories of being told what to do. Not the content of those instructions. The *feeling* of complying. Did it feel safe? Did saying yes mean you'd be accepted, praised, kept close? Did saying no ever result in coldness, disappointment, withdrawal?

For a lot of us, particularly those who grew up in homes where expressing needs was discouraged or punished, "yes" became a survival strategy. It signaled you were good. Compliant. Not a problem. The internal message wasn't *this is good for me*—it was *doing what I'm told keeps me safe*. And that pattern doesn't just evaporate with age. It gets wired into your nervous system, becomes automatic. An adult hands you an orange and your hands open before you've consciously decided whether you have room for it.

Here's what happens physiologically when you override those signals consistently: you train your body to stop sending them, or at least to raise the threshold for what counts as distress. You become desensitized to your own discomfort. Meanwhile, you grow dependent on external stimulation—on *doing* things—to regulate your emotional state. Anxiety drives you to overcommit. Overcommitment depletes your resources. Depletion increases anxiety. The loop tightens.

Cortisol—the stress hormone—stays elevated longer. Your vagus nerve, which governs the parasympathetic "rest and digest" system, gets less practice shifting you down from high alert. You're essentially stuck in mild stress response, perpetually. Not enough to collapse. Just enough to erode you slowly.

It's not that saying yes is inherently destructive. It's the lack of *choice* in it. The automaticity. When you're running on autopilot, your prefrontal cortex—the part responsible for rational thought, for weighing whether this request aligns with your values or capacity—isn't fully engaged. You're operating from older, reactive wiring. And in that state, you're not assessing. You're just reacting.

So how do you break free without resorting to blunt refusals that feel like tearing the social fabric?

The answer isn't learning to say no, exactly. It's learning to insert space between the request and your response. A pause. A moment of internal inventory before your mouth opens and says yes.

This is about reclaiming agency. Not selfishness. Not self-indulgence. Sustainability. A depleted resource offers nothing to anyone. A constantly overflowing cup spills everywhere and nourishes no one.

Mark learned this the hard way.

He was a project manager at a mid-sized tech firm. Thirtysomething, competent, perpetually volunteering for extra tasks even when his plate was already full to cracking. From the outside he looked like the model employee—efficient, reliable, always willing. Privately he was fighting debilitating fatigue and an irritability so sharp it startled him. He'd snap at his partner over minor things—dishes in the sink, a forgotten errand—and then lie awake at night hating himself for it.

When we started working together, I didn't tell him to stop volunteering. That would've triggered immediate anxiety. The thought of saying no felt more dangerous than the exhaustion. So instead we focused on building in a pause.

The technique was absurdly simple: the three-breath buffer.

When presented with a request, Mark was instructed to take three slow, deliberate breaths before responding. Not to formulate an answer during those breaths. Just to *feel* what was happening in his body. Was his jaw clenching? Shoulders rising? Where was the sensation of overwhelm showing up?

Three breaths. That's it.

He hated it at first. "It feels rude," he said. "Like I'm making them wait. Like I'm being difficult."

I asked him what "difficult" meant to him. He thought about it. "Like I'm not... eager. Like I'm not grateful for the opportunity."

We sat with that. The belief that hesitation equals ingratitude. That a pause might communicate incompetence or reluctance. We reframed it as professional courtesy: "You want to deliver quality work. You can't do that running on fumes. Taking a moment to assess your capacity isn't difficult—it's ensuring you can fulfill the commitment effectively."

It took weeks before it felt even remotely natural. But Mark started noticing shifts. The three-breath buffer allowed him to *feel* his physical limits before hitting the wall. He started responding differently: "Let me check my current priorities and get back to you." Or: "That sounds interesting, but I'm committed to X and Y this week. Could we discuss it next week?"

Not refusals. Boundary statements. Delivered politely, professionally. And crucially, they allowed him to maintain control without triggering the panic that came with a flat "no."

The practice extends beyond work. Social invitations. Family obligations. Small requests from friends. It's not about rigid rules or becoming a hermit. It's about honoring your internal needs. Recognizing that every yes costs you—your energy, your time, your bandwidth. And understanding that protecting those resources isn't selfish. It's essential.

There will be slips. Times you fall back into the old pattern, say yes before you've thought it through, feel the tower of oranges wobble again. That's fine. Expected. Progress doesn't move in a straight line. The key is noticing, gently redirecting your attention, and remembering that setbacks aren't failures—they're data.

But even with this awareness, even with tools like the three-breath buffer and a gentler view of mistakes, there's often something deeper at work. Something pulling you back into overcommitment that's less about specific requests and more about what drives the relentless striving itself.

That something is energy.

Not in a mystical sense. In a literal, physiological sense. Your body runs on fuel. Glucose powers your brain. Every decision you make, every task you switch between, every emotion you suppress—all of it burns through that fuel. And for those of us wired toward high-functioning anxiety, we've become dangerously skilled at ignoring depletion until we're running on fumes.

Think about a normal Tuesday. Not the crises or big projects. Just the constant hum of small demands. Replying to emails while trying to focus on a report. Saying yes to covering a colleague's shift because "it's easier than explaining why I can't." Mentally rehearsing a difficult conversation beforehand, then replaying it afterward to analyze every word. None of these feel exhausting in isolation. Cumulatively? They're draining you dry.

You might not even register it as exhaustion. You just find yourself inexplicably irritable by evening. Unable to focus on simple tasks. Numb. Snapping at people you love over nothing.

What's happening: your prefrontal cortex—the part managing executive functions like planning, impulse control, and yes, managing anxiety—is energy-intensive. Constant activation, even low-level, depletes glucose reserves. Your adrenal system stays subtly engaged, releasing cortisol. Helpful in acute situations. Corrosive when chronic. You're stuck in prolonged mild stress response, and it wears you down.

The problem isn't *doing* things. It's doing too much with insufficient recovery. Spending energy on things that don't matter while neglecting what does.

This is where boundaries stop being about blocking access and start being about directing flow. You're not preventing things from reaching you. You're choosing where your energy goes.

I know "boundaries" feels loaded. Conjures images of confrontation, guilt. Especially if you've spent decades prioritizing everyone else's needs. So let's reframe it: boundaries aren't what you *prevent*. They're what you actively allow to receive your finite resources. And recognizing those resources *are* finite requires a shift—understanding that saying yes to everything is inherently saying no to something else. Usually yourself.

A tool that helps: task triage.

Not about eliminating tasks entirely (though sometimes, yes). About categorizing them by energy cost and actual importance. Picture a grid. Two axes: Importance (high/low) and Energy Cost (high/low).

High Importance, Low Energy: Non-negotiables that don't deplete you. Tasks aligned with your values that you can handle without draining the tank. Prioritize these.

High Importance, High Energy: These need planning. Can you break them into smaller pieces? Delegate parts? Schedule them during peak energy windows?

Low Importance, Low Energy: Filler tasks. Don't move the needle but aren't overly draining. Do these only with surplus energy, or eliminate them.

Low Importance, High Energy: This is where the leaks are. Things you do out of habit, obligation, fear of disappointing someone. These need to be actively minimized or cut.

Amelia figured this out the hard way.

She was a marketing manager, early thirties, classic high-functioning profile—driven, successful, terrified of falling behind. She volunteered for extra projects constantly. Responded to emails within minutes, even on vacation. Spent hours perfecting presentations that rarely made it past the first review.

She described feeling "on" all the time. Exhausted. Resentful, though she couldn't articulate toward what.

We started by mapping her week, not in tasks completed but energy expended. The pattern became obvious quickly: she was operating almost entirely in the High Importance, High Energy quadrant. Taking on complex projects that *felt* critical to the team, even when they weren't her responsibility. Worse, she filled the gaps with Low Importance, High Energy work—rewriting colleagues' reports "because it's faster to do it myself," preemptively fixing problems that hadn't materialized.

The resistance to setting boundaries wasn't about the tasks. It was the belief underneath: that she needed to prove her value through constant activity. She feared looking incompetent or lazy if she didn't take on everything offered.

We reframed it. Not about being nice or mean. About responsible resource management.

We practiced phrasing requests as questions that shifted the dynamic. Instead of "I can't rewrite that report," she'd say: "That's a thorough draft! Have you considered running it by Sarah in editing? She's great with detail." Instead of immediate email responses, she batched replies to specific times.

It wasn't magic. There was discomfort. Anxiety surged when she resisted the urge to "fix" things, to say yes reflexively. But Amelia started noticing something: her energy didn't plummet throughout the day. She had bandwidth for tasks that actually mattered. She completed them with more focus, more creativity. The resentment faded, replaced by agency.

The key wasn't eliminating demands—that's impossible. It was choosing where to invest energy, protecting reserves for what genuinely needed them, redirecting flow away from what drained without delivering returns. And learning that sometimes letting something go isn't weakness. It's self-preservation.

But knowing you *should* protect your energy and actually doing it when someone's standing in front of you asking for help—those are different things entirely.

The difficulty for those of us navigating high-functioning anxiety isn't identifying boundaries. It's enforcing them. We know when we're overextended. We can feel it. What tangles us up is the internal pressure to appear helpful, reliable, indispensable. The fear that asserting a limit will disappoint someone, damage a relationship, confirm we're selfish.

Physiologically, anticipating having to say no activates your sympathetic nervous system. Not full fight-or-flight, but low-grade: heart rate increases, breath shallows, muscles tense. Your body prepares to defend against perceived threat. Not because the request itself is dangerous—because you've learned that asserting needs risks disapproval. Cognitively, you get the cascade of "what ifs." *What if they think I'm lazy? What if they ask someone else who does it better? What if they're disappointed?*

These thoughts aren't rational. They feel real. And they powerfully influence behavior.

A technique that helps: the Broken Record with a Buffer.

The "broken record" part means politely repeating your limited availability without endless explanations. People prone to high-functioning anxiety over-explain, hoping to preemptively diffuse upset. This just opens negotiation—and drains more energy. The "buffer" is a softening phrase used *before* you state the boundary, acknowledging the request and validating the need. It doesn't change the limit. It communicates respect.

Example: Liam, a project manager, constantly gets asked to review documents outside his responsibilities. He's good at it, so people gravitate toward him even when their own teammates should handle it. A colleague, Sarah, emails asking him to review a complex marketing report.

Instead of "Sure, I'll take a look when I have time" (vague, invites pressure) or "I'm really swamped, so no" (abrupt), Liam replies:

"Hi Sarah, I appreciate you thinking of me for this. It sounds like an important report. Right now my priority is finalizing the Henderson proposal, which has a tight deadline. Because of that, I won't be able to give your report the thorough review it deserves. Perhaps Mark in marketing would have capacity? He's done similar reviews before."

Notice: Liam acknowledges the request. Validates its importance. States his current priority. Explains why he can't help—tied to existing obligation, not general busyness. Offers a solution. Doesn't apologize. Just explains.

If Sarah pushes back—"Oh, it won't take long"—Liam repeats calmly: "I understand, but my focus needs to be on Henderson right now." If she says "No one understands this project like you do," he might say: "I'm confident Mark will provide valuable feedback."

He repeats the core message without debating.

This isn't dishonesty or avoiding responsibility. It's strategic allocation. Protecting yourself from chronic overwhelm. And here's the thing a lot of people with high-functioning anxiety miss: self-care isn't elaborate rituals—long baths, expensive massages. It's quiet, consistent boundary enforcement. The unglamorous work of saying "not now" or "not me."

Another technique: Time Banking.

Acknowledge the request, propose a trade or delay. "I'm happy to help with that next week, after I finish the Peterson report." Or: "I can fit that in if you could possibly take on the data entry for the Johnson account?"

Doesn't always work. Sometimes the other person can't reciprocate. But it subtly shifts the dynamic from one-sided obligation to equitable exchange. Not about keeping score. About establishing that your time has value.

Maya, an architect, found herself constantly proofreading colleagues' grant applications on top of her own demanding workload. She wanted to support them. But she was perpetually exhausted. Previously she'd agree automatically, then spend late nights resentfully correcting grammar while her own deadlines loomed.

Using time banking, when David asked for help with his latest application, Maya responded: "David, I'm glad you asked. That's a crucial application. I'm deep in the Riverside project this week, but I could look at it next Monday if that works. Alternatively, if you're on a tight timeline, would you have time to compile the reference list for my museum proposal? That would free me up to review yours sooner."

David ended up doing the reference list. Not because Maya manipulated him, but because she framed it as mutual support rather than one-way assistance. She helped him. He helped her. Both benefited.

The shift isn't about becoming transactional or cold. It's about recognizing that sustainable relationships—professional or personal—require reciprocity. And that you're allowed to need things too.

One more approach, particularly useful with chronic boundary-pushers: the Preemptive Redirect.

Some people will keep asking because you keep saying yes. They've learned you're a reliable resource. Changing that pattern requires consistency and clarity. Instead of waiting for the request, you address the pattern directly.

Suppose your manager habitually assigns you last-minute projects, assuming you'll accommodate. Rather than addressing it in the moment when emotions are high and you're already overwhelmed, schedule a brief conversation: "I wanted to touch base about project timelines. I've noticed I often receive assignments late in the cycle, which makes it difficult to deliver my best work. Moving forward, would it be possible to get at least 48 hours' notice for new projects? That way I can plan effectively and ensure quality."

You're not refusing work. You're setting a structural boundary that protects your capacity. Most reasonable managers will accommodate—they want quality work too. And if they don't? That's information. That tells you something about whether this environment respects your limits, which is itself valuable data.

I'll be honest: I've struggled with this one. For years I'd agree to keynotes with two weeks' notice, tell myself it was fine, then spend those two weeks in low-grade panic trying to prepare while managing everything else. The talks were fine. I delivered. But the cost was brutal—sleep deprivation, snapping at my family, a persistent knot of anxiety. It took my partner saying, quite gently, "You know you're allowed to ask for more time, right?" for me to realize I'd never even considered it an option. I thought the request *was* the deadline. I've since implemented a firm "minimum six weeks' notice" policy for speaking engagements, and the relief is... substantial. I'm a better speaker with adequate prep time. The talks are stronger. And I don't spend a month resenting the commitment.

These techniques—the three-breath buffer, task triage, the broken record, time banking, preemptive redirects—they're not about constructing fortress walls around yourself. They're about creating a sustainable rhythm. Protecting the energy required to do work that matters, to be present for people you care about, to have something left at the end of the day besides exhaustion.

It takes practice. There will be backslides. Moments when the old pattern reasserts itself and you say yes before you've thought it through. That's okay. It's expected. You're rewiring deeply ingrained responses. Be patient with yourself.

But here's what I want you to sit with: every time you say yes when you want to say no, when you override your body's signals and add another orange to the stack, you're not just depleting your energy. You're teaching yourself that your needs don't matter. That other people's comfort is more important than your well-being. That you're only valuable when you're producing, accommodating, giving.

And that's not true.

You're valuable because you exist. Your energy is finite and precious. Protecting it isn't selfish—it's the baseline requirement for building a life that doesn't constantly feel like it's on the verge of collapse.

So the next time someone hands you an orange and you feel your hands start to shake, I want you to pause. Take three breaths. Feel what's happening in your body. And then—gently, firmly—decide whether you have room for it. Not whether you *should* make room. Whether you *actually* have room.

You might surprise yourself with the answer.

And if the tower wobbles a bit because you didn't take it, because you chose to protect your own structure instead of accommodating one more thing—well. That tells you something too. About whose job it is to keep the oranges from falling. And whether you've been carrying weight that was never yours to hold in the first place.

Chapter 6: Interrupting the Internal Critic

I watched a client once spend forty-seven minutes rewriting a single text message to her sister. Not a work email. Not a breakup text. Just: "Can't make dinner Tuesday, let's do next week?"

She'd type it, delete it, rephrase, second-guess the tone, worry the exclamation point seemed too casual or the period too cold. When I finally asked what she was afraid would happen if she just sent the first version, she looked at me like I'd suggested she show up to dinner naked. "She'll think I don't care," she said.

Then, quieter: "She'll be right."

That's the thing about the internal critic nobody tells you. It doesn't announce itself with a megaphone. It doesn't scream "YOU'RE WORTHLESS" while you're trying to make toast. It's far more insidious than that. It's the reason you reread emails six times before hitting send. It's why you apologize for asking questions in meetings. It's the voice that turns "I made a mistake" into "I am a mistake"—and it does it so smoothly you don't even notice the switch.

For years I told myself I didn't have this problem. I wasn't anxious, I was thorough. I wasn't people-pleasing, I was considerate. I wasn't beating myself up, I was holding myself to high standards.

And honestly? That's exactly what the critic wants you to think. Because the moment you recognize it as anxiety, you might actually do something about it. Better to disguise it as professionalism, as conscientiousness, as caring what people think—because who wants to be the person who doesn't care?

I remember sitting in a supervision session early in my career, listening to myself explain why I'd spent three hours preparing for a fifty-minute therapy appointment. My supervisor just looked at me. "That's not preparation," she said. "That's terror dressed up as competence." I laughed it off. But she was right. I wasn't preparing—I was trying to anxiety-proof the session, to control every possible direction the conversation might go so I'd never be caught off guard, never look like I didn't know what I was doing. As if that's even possible. As if therapy—or life—works that way.

The internal critic operates like a radio station you never consciously tuned to but somehow can't turn off. And here's what makes it particularly brutal for high-functioning anxiety: the station plays a very specific format. Not the dramatic, catastrophic stuff—those tracks are too obvious, too easy to dismiss. No, this station specializes in the subtle hits. The "you should have known better" after a minor miscommunication. The "everyone else manages this effortlessly" when you're struggling with something totally normal. The endless loop of "what will they think?" that plays underneath nearly every decision.

What's actually happening in your brain during all this—and I say this knowing full well it won't make it stop, but sometimes understanding the mechanism helps—is that your threat-detection system has gotten confused about what constitutes a threat. Missing a typo in an email is being processed with roughly the same neurological alarm as missing a step on a ladder. Your amygdala can't tell the difference between social embarrassment and physical danger, so it treats both like emergencies. Which means your baseline stress hormones stay elevated. Not spiking into full panic—that would be too noticeable—but humming along at a level just high enough to keep you perpetually braced for impact.

The exhaustion that comes from this isn't the satisfying kind you get after a hard workout or a productive day. It's the bone-deep weariness of having run a marathon in your own head before you've even gotten out of bed.

Because the critic doesn't take days off. It doesn't clock out at five. It's there when you're falling asleep, replaying that thing you said three hours ago and composing better versions you should have said instead.

Here's what it costs you—and I mean *really* costs you, not in some abstract "oh that's unfortunate" way:

You stop trusting yourself. Every decision becomes a referendum. Should I speak up in this meeting? Should I order what I actually want at the restaurant or what seems least complicated? Should I wear this or will people think I'm trying too hard—or not trying hard enough? The critic has convinced you that your first instinct is probably wrong, so you second-guess everything. Then you third-guess it. Then you're so far removed from what you actually wanted in the first place that you can't remember what that even was.

I've watched this play out in dozens of ways. The lawyer who brings three backup outfits to the office because she can't trust her morning judgment. The teacher who rehearses casual hallway small talk in his car before walking into school. The parent who googles "normal amount of screen time" seventeen different ways because she can't trust her own read of what her kid needs.

You become a curator of other people's potential reactions. You're not living your life; you're managing their theoretical experience of you. Before you post something on social media, you're not thinking "do I like this?"—you're running simulations of how seventeen different people might interpret it. You phrase texts in ways that preemptively defend against criticism that no one was actually going to levy. You're exhausting yourself managing a conversation that hasn't happened with a person who isn't even thinking about you.

Your relationships suffer in ways that are hard to name. Because you're so busy monitoring your own performance—Am I being a good friend right now? Did I ask enough questions? Did I talk too much about myself?—that you're not actually present. People can feel that. They can sense when you're performing connection rather than experiencing it. And the tragic irony is that the harder you try to be liked, the more distant you become, because there's no actual *you* in the interaction anymore. Just a carefully managed avatar designed to avoid criticism.

You abandon things that matter to you.

Not dramatically—you don't storm out or make declarations. You just quietly stop trying. Because the critic has made it clear: if you're not going to be excellent at something, why bother? Can't commit to practicing guitar unless you can guarantee you'll be good at it. Can't try that creative project unless you're certain it won't be embarrassing. Better to not try than to try and confirm the critic's worst suspicions about you. So you end up living smaller and smaller, in the ever-shrinking space of things you're already confident you can do well.

And maybe the cruelest cost: you're never actually satisfied when things go well. Someone compliments your work and instead of feeling pleased, you're immediately scanning for the ulterior motive, the hidden criticism, the ways you could have done it better. You hit a goal you've been working toward and the critic says, "Took you long enough" or "Anyone could have done that" or my personal favorite: "Now you have to maintain it."

There's no finish line. There's no moment of rest. The critic has convinced you that your worth is always provisional, always subject to the next performance review.

I see this most clearly in Marcus, though that's not his real name. Venture capital analyst, the kind of guy who reads three books a week and somehow makes it to a 6 AM cycling class and still gets to the office before anyone else. Objectively successful by every metric his firm measures. But the first time he came to see me, he described feeling like he was "constantly failing in slow motion."

Here's what that looked like in practice: He'd finish a deal—the kind that makes headlines, the kind that gets you promoted—and his first thought would be about the one question during the pitch meeting he'd fumbled. Not fumbled badly. Just answered in a way that felt less crisp than it could have been. He'd replay that thirty-second exchange for days, composing better responses, sharper comebacks, imagining the respect he *would* have earned if only he'd been quicker.

Or: he'd be in a partner meeting, ostensibly participating, but actually running a parallel narrative in his head about how his contribution compared to everyone else's. Was he talking too much? Not enough? Did that comment land or did people think it was obvious? He'd leave those meetings so depleted he'd need to sit in his car for ten minutes before driving home, and he couldn't even articulate why. Nothing bad had happened. He'd just spent ninety minutes in a mental boxing match with himself.

The critic's voice in his case wasn't even particularly harsh. It wasn't calling him an idiot or a failure. It was worse than that—it was reasonable. It sounded like prudence, like professional development, like healthy self-assessment. "Just making sure I'm on top of things," he'd say. "Just being thorough."

And that's the real trick, isn't it? The critic has learned to disguise itself as your ally. As the voice that keeps you sharp, that prevents you from getting complacent, that pushes you to be your best self. It's very convincing.

Until you start paying attention to what it actually says, and how often it says it.

So here's the first move—and I'm not going to pretend this is easy, because it's not, but it's necessary: you have to start noticing the critic as a separate voice. Not as "you." Not as "truth." As a pattern of thought that your brain has learned to run, the same way it's learned to tie your shoes or navigate to work without conscious attention.

This is harder than it sounds because the critic has been running for so long it feels like your natural inner monologue. But it's not. It's a habit. A deeply ingrained one, sure, but a habit nonetheless. And the first step in changing any habit is recognizing when it's happening.

Pay attention to the tone first, not even the content. Is it harsh? Sarcastic? Disappointed? Does it sound like someone you'd actually want to take advice from, or does it sound like that one person at every job who makes every conversation feel like a performance review?

Then notice the themes. What does your critic obsess over? Performance at work? Your appearance? How you come across socially? Whether you're doing enough, being enough, achieving enough? Is there a specific trigger—certain people, situations, times of day when the critic gets particularly loud?

Marcus's trigger, once he started paying attention, was feedback. Any feedback. Someone would praise a presentation he'd given and his immediate internal response was: "They're being polite. They probably have notes they're not sharing. They think the next one needs to be even better." Positive feedback got processed as a threat because it raised the bar, gave him a new standard to fail to meet. He wasn't hearing "good job"—he was hearing "don't screw up next time."

The critic would frame everything as risk management. *Just triple-check those numbers. Just make sure you didn't miss anything. Just think through how this could go wrong.* It sounded responsible. It sounded like due diligence. What it actually was: a relentless audit of his competence, a constant suggestion that his first effort was probably flawed, that he couldn't trust his own judgment without running it through seventeen verification loops.

Once he started labeling it—"okay, that's the critic, not me"—something shifted. Not dramatically. Not overnight. But he'd catch himself about to rewrite an email for the fifth time and he'd pause. *There it is again.* That voice insisting this had to be perfect, that someone would judge him for a misplaced comma, that his credibility hung on every word. And instead of automatically obeying it, he'd just… observe it. "My brain is doing the thing where it insists this email is a catastrophe waiting to happen."

The email was fine. It was always fine. But the critic had convinced him that "fine" was unacceptable, that anything less than optimized was failure. So he'd been optimizing himself into exhaustion, one minor decision at a time.

What you're doing when you label the thought—when you say "that's the critic" instead of just experiencing it as reality—is called cognitive defusion. Which is a therapy term that sounds more complicated than it is. All it means is: creating some distance between yourself and your thoughts. Recognizing that thoughts are mental events, not facts. That your brain produces thousands of thoughts a day, and most of them are just… noise. You don't have to believe them all. You don't have to obey them all.

Think of it like this: Your mind is a radio that never turns off, constantly playing different stations. Some channels are useful—the one that reminds you to eat lunch, to call your mom on her birthday, to check the stove before you leave. Some are just background static. And some—like the internal critic—play the same terrible song on repeat, and somehow you've gotten convinced you have to keep listening.

Defusion is realizing you can change the station. Or at least turn the volume down.

You can't control what song comes on next—your brain is going to produce critical thoughts, probably for the rest of your life—but you can control how much authority you give those thoughts. Whether you let them dictate your behavior or whether you just let them be background noise while you get on with what you were doing.

One technique that sounds absolutely ridiculous until you try it: say the critical thought out loud in a cartoon voice. Seriously. The critic shows up with "You're going to mess this up"—repeat it like Elmo. Or a robot. Or that one uncle who thinks he's hilarious. The point isn't to mock the thought, exactly. It's to disrupt the automatic emotional weight you give it. Because we tend to treat our internal dialogue as this authoritative broadcast, capital-T Truth handed down from on high. But when you hear "You're inadequate" in

SpongeBob's voice, it's pretty hard to take it seriously.

I felt like an idiot the first time I tried this. I was preparing for a workshop and the critic was in full form—*You're going to forget something important. Someone's going to ask a question you can't answer. They're going to realize you don't actually know what you're doing.* And I remembered telling a client about the cartoon voice technique the week before, so I figured I should at least try my own advice. I locked my office door (because even alone I was self-conscious about this) and repeated the thought in the voice of Yoda. "Forget something important, you will. Realize you don't know what you're doing, they will."

It was so absurd I actually laughed. And that break—that tiny moment of absurdity—was enough to let me see the thought for what it was. Not a prophecy. Not wisdom. Just my brain doing its anxious thing, trying to protect me from humiliation by preemptively humiliating me in private. Real helpful, brain.

Another approach: "Thank your mind." The critic pipes up—"Everyone's going to think you're an idiot"—and you respond, internally, "Thanks for that input, brain." Not sarcastically (though it'll feel sarcastic at first). But as a genuine acknowledgment that your brain is trying to help, even if its methods are terrible. It's trying to protect you from embarrassment, from failure, from rejection. It's just doing it in the most counterproductive way possible, like a very anxious, very bad life coach.

I tried this once after completely blanking during a workshop I was running. Mid-sentence, lost my train of thought, stood there in front of forty people with my mouth open like a landed fish. My immediate internal response was the critic's greatest hits: *Professional disaster. They're all judging you. You're not qualified to be teaching this.* And somewhere in the middle of that spiral I remembered my own advice and thought, *Oh, thanks brain. Very helpful. Really nailing the supportive coach energy right now.*

It didn't make the embarrassment disappear. But it did make the critic's voice a little less… totalizing. Like, yes, I blanked. That happened. It was awkward. But it wasn't actually a referendum on my worth as a human or my competence as a therapist. It was just a thing that happened, the kind of thing that happens to everyone who speaks in public, and my brain was making it into a catastrophe because that's what anxious brains do.

The goal isn't to never have critical thoughts. That's not realistic and honestly, some self-assessment is useful. The goal is to change your relationship with those thoughts—to recognize the critic as one voice among many, not the ultimate authority on who you are and what you're capable of.

Let's say you're in a meeting and you ask a question that feels obvious the second it leaves your mouth. The critic immediately jumps in: *Everyone knows this already. They think you're unprepared. They're wondering why you're even here.*

Old pattern: believe the critic, spend the rest of the meeting mentally composing apologies and trying to prove you're not an idiot, leave feeling like you've confirmed your own incompetence.

New pattern: *Okay, there's the critic. Running its usual script about how everyone's judging me.* You don't argue with it. You don't try to convince it the question was fine. You just label it—"that's a critical thought"—and shift your attention back to the actual meeting. Which, if you were paying attention instead of managing your internal crisis, might reveal that no one else thought the question was stupid. Someone might even say, "Good question, I was wondering that too."

This takes practice. The critic has been running its show for years, maybe decades. It's not going to pack up quietly just because you've started labeling it. Some days you'll catch yourself three hours into a shame spiral before you remember you have tools for this.

That's normal. You're not failing at defusion. You're just learning a new skill, and all new skills feel clumsy at first.

Another thing that helps: write down what the critic actually says. Not paraphrased. Not summarized. Word for word, the way you'd transcribe dialogue in a play.

"You're going to embarrass yourself." "No one wants to hear what you have to say." "You should have figured this out by now." "Everyone else is handling this better than you."

When you see it written out like that, you start to notice patterns. The critic has about six scripts that it runs on loop, just remixed for different situations. It's not creative. It's not insightful. It's repetitive and mean and honestly kind of boring once you see the formula.

One client did this for a week and came back to session genuinely angry. "I can't believe I've been letting *this* run my life," she said. She'd filled three pages with variations on "you're not good enough" and "people are disappointed in you." Three pages of the same attack, just wearing different outfits. And when she could see it all laid out in her own handwriting, it stopped feeling like truth and started feeling like… harassment. Like someone following her around all day whispering the worst possible interpretation of every moment. She wouldn't tolerate that from another person. Why was she tolerating it from her own mind?

Talk to someone you trust about this—a friend, a partner, a therapist. Sometimes just saying the critical thought out loud exposes how distorted it is. "I sent an email with a typo and now I'm convinced my boss thinks I'm incompetent" sounds a lot more irrational when you hear it in your own voice in someone else's living room than it does echoing in your head at 2 AM.

But even without external validation, you have more power here than you think. You can start interrupting the playlist. You can notice the song, name it, and choose not to let it run your day.

The woman who spent forty-seven minutes on that text to her sister? She eventually sent version one. Turns out her sister didn't think she was uncaring. Didn't even notice the lack of exclamation point. Just texted back "No worries, next week works!" The catastrophe existed only in the space between her and the critic.

And Marcus—he started sending emails after one revision instead of five. The sky didn't fall. No one called him out for sloppy work. In fact, he got faster responses because people weren't waiting three hours for him to craft the perfect message. The thing he'd been protecting himself against by over-checking, over-preparing, over-monitoring? It wasn't actually a threat. It was just the critic, insisting it was.

Here's where this gets interesting, though—and by interesting I mean uncomfortable. Because once you start labeling the critic, once you start seeing it as a pattern instead of truth, you can't help but ask: *Where did this come from?*

The critic doesn't just materialize out of nowhere. It learned what to say. It learned what standards to hold you to, what failures to obsess over, what kinds of success don't count. And it learned that from somewhere. From someone.

Maybe it sounds like a parent. That particular tone of disappointment when you brought home a B instead of an A, the way love felt conditional on achievement. Or maybe it sounds like a teacher who pointed out what was wrong before acknowledging what was right, training you to always scan for the flaw first. Maybe it's an ex who cataloged your shortcomings so thoroughly you started doing the cataloging yourself, just to stay ahead of it. Or maybe it doesn't sound like anyone specific—it's just the background hum of a culture that treats anxiety as productivity, that celebrates the grind, that insists if you're not exhausted you're not trying hard enough.

For Marcus, it sounded like his father. A man who'd built a real estate empire from nothing and couldn't understand why his son would choose a "soft" career like venture capital instead of something "real" like construction or manufacturing. Never mind that Marcus was making three times what his father ever had—it didn't count because it wasn't the *right kind* of success. The critic had his father's voice, his father's dismissiveness, his father's unspoken message that whatever Marcus did, it would never quite be enough.

And here's the thing: even when you know where the voice came from, even when you can trace it back to a specific person or moment, that doesn't automatically make it go away. Knowledge isn't the same as healing. But it does give you something to push against. It lets you ask: *Is this actually my standard, or is this someone else's standard I'm still trying to meet?*

Because a lot of what the critic says isn't even about you. It's about someone else's unmet expectations, their projections, their own anxieties that they handed down like a family heirloom. And you've been carrying it. Polishing it. Trying to make it fit. When maybe the real question is: why are you still trying to meet standards set by someone who didn't understand what you needed in the first place?

I'm not saying you blame your parents or your ex or your third-grade teacher for every critical thought you have. That's too easy, and it's also kind of useless. You're an adult now. The critic is *yours*, even if you didn't choose it. But there's something powerful in recognizing that the voice telling you you're not good enough might not be telling the truth—it might just be repeating a truth someone else believed, once, that you absorbed before you knew you could refuse it.

So what happens when you start refusing it?

Not all at once. Not in some dramatic confrontation where you banish the critic forever. But in small, specific moments. You notice the critical thought—"I should be better at this by now"—and you ask: *According to who? What timeline am I measuring myself against?* And often, if you're honest, the answer is: a completely arbitrary one. A timeline that doesn't account for the actual complexity of your life, your circumstances, the fact that you're learning as you go like everyone else.

Here's what that looks like in practice:

The critic says: "You should have known better." You ask: "Based on what information? What was I supposed to know that I didn't?" Often the answer is: nothing. You made the best decision you could with the information you had at the time. The critic is just running the highlight reel of your mistakes with the benefit of hindsight, pretending you should have had access to information you only learned later.

The critic says: "Everyone else is managing this fine." You ask: "Am I actually comparing myself to real people, or to the imaginary highlight reel they show the world?" Because the critic never compares you to the full, messy, complicated reality of other people's lives. It compares you to the curated version, the competence performance, the parts they're willing to let you see. You're comparing your behind-the-scenes to everyone else's public persona, and then beating yourself up for not measuring up to a standard that doesn't even exist.

The critic says: "You're not doing enough." You ask: "Enough for what? What's the actual goal here?" And sometimes—not always, but sometimes—you realize there isn't one. The goal is just "more." Be more productive. Achieve more. Optimize more. There's no finish line, no moment when the critic will say "okay, you did enough, you can rest now." Because the critic isn't interested in your wellbeing. It's interested in keeping you in motion, in preventing the imagined catastrophe of someone thinking you're lazy or unambitious or—god forbid—average.

I had to learn this the hard way. A few years ago I was running a private practice, teaching workshops, writing articles, saying yes to every podcast interview and speaking opportunity that came my way. I was tired all the time but I kept telling myself it was fine, this is just what building a career looks like, everyone hustles like this. The critic told me I couldn't slow down because then people would forget about me, opportunities would dry up, I'd prove I wasn't actually that serious about my work.

Then I got shingles. At thirty-four. Which, if you're not familiar, is basically your body's way of waving a giant red flag and screaming "we need to talk about your stress levels." And even lying in bed, unable to move without pain shooting across my ribs, the critic was *still going. You're going to lose clients. People are going to think you're unreliable. You should be working through this.*

My doctor—a woman I barely knew but will be forever grateful for—looked at me during a follow-up appointment and said, "You know this isn't sustainable, right? Like, you understand your body just forced you to stop because you wouldn't choose to stop on your own?"

I nodded. I knew. I'd been ignoring it, but I knew.

"So what are you going to do differently?" she asked.

And I had no idea. Because the critic had convinced me that "sustainable" was just another word for "settling." That boundaries were for people who didn't care enough, didn't want it badly enough. That rest was what you earned after you'd proven yourself, not something you needed just to function like a human being.

It took months—honestly, it's still taking time—to untangle that. To recognize that the voice telling me I had to earn rest wasn't wisdom, it was just anxiety wearing a productivity costume. That the standards I was holding myself to weren't leading me toward any actual goal, they were just keeping me too busy to notice I was miserable.

So here's what I want you to try, and I know this is going to feel weird, maybe even wrong, but try it anyway:

For the next week, just notice. Don't try to fix anything yet, don't try to argue with the critic, don't even try to defuse the thoughts. Just pay attention. When does the critic show up? What does it say? What's the tone, the theme, the trigger?

Carry a small notebook or use your phone. When you catch the critic in action, write down: - The situation (meeting, email, conversation, etc.) - The exact thought ("I'm going to mess this up") - The feeling in your body (tight chest, stomach drop, jaw clenched)

Don't analyze it. Don't judge yourself for having the thought. Just collect the data. You're a researcher studying your own mind, and you're gathering evidence about how this pattern actually operates.

You might be surprised by how automatic it is, how much of your mental real estate it's occupying without you ever consciously inviting it in. You might notice the critic shows up most when you're tired, or when you're around specific people, or in specific situations. You might realize it has the same three or four scripts it cycles through, regardless of circumstances.

And once you've noticed it—once you've started to see the critic as a pattern instead of as truth—then you can start asking a different kind of question.

Not "Is this thought true?" but "Is this thought useful?"

Not "Am I really failing?" but "Who decided those were the standards I had to meet in the first place?"

Because here's what almost no one talks about: the critic isn't just running on its own. It's being fueled by something deeper. Beliefs about what you *should* be doing, who you *should* be. And a lot of those beliefs? You didn't choose them. They were handed to you—by your family, your culture, the version of success you absorbed before you were old enough to question it.

The critic is vicious, yes. But it's vicious in service of rules you never actually agreed to follow.

So what happens when you start questioning those rules? When you ask not just "how do I manage the critic?" but "why am I listening to it at all?"

That's not a rhetorical question. And the answer—when you let yourself actually consider it, not just deflect or rationalize or explain it away—might tell you something important. Not about your competence or your worth or whether you're doing enough. But about what you've been running from, and what might be waiting if you finally stopped.

Chapter 7: Social Anxiety in Performance Spaces

Adele once described her pre-show ritual in a way that stuck with me. Before walking onstage to perform for tens of thousands of people, she would sometimes vomit from sheer terror. Not nerves. Terror. Here's a woman who's sold over 120 million records, won fifteen Grammys, and whose voice has moved millions—and still, the anxiety came. She'd finish being sick, wipe her mouth, and walk out to deliver a flawless performance. That's high-functioning anxiety in its most visible form: producing excellence while internally dissolving.

Most of us won't ever perform at the O2 Arena. But we know that feeling. The presentation that goes smoothly while your heart hammers against your ribs. The dinner party where you're charming and attentive while monitoring every word that leaves your mouth. The job interview where you nail every answer while a voice in your head catalogs every micro-expression on the interviewer's face, searching for signs of disapproval.

I spent years believing this was just how conscientious people operated. That the internal monitoring—the constant self-surveillance—was the *reason* I performed well. Strip away the anxiety, I figured, and I'd lose my edge. I'd become complacent. Sloppy.

That's a lie anxiety tells to keep itself employed.

The truth is messier. Yes, you can function with anxiety. You can deliver the presentation, host the dinner, ace the interview. But you're doing it while operating a piece of machinery that's actively working against you. It's like driving with the parking brake engaged—you'll get where you're going, but you're burning out parts you can't easily replace.

What Your Body Actually Does When It Thinks You're Being Judged

Here's what happens in those moments when you feel observed, evaluated, judged. Your amygdala—the brain's ancient alarm system—doesn't distinguish between a genuine threat and a perceived social one. It doesn't care that you're giving a quarterly report, not fleeing a predator. When you anticipate judgment, when you sense the possibility of looking foolish or incompetent, your body mobilizes the same stress response it would for physical danger. Heart rate increases. Breathing becomes shallow. Muscles tense. Blood flow shifts away from your digestive system and toward your limbs—preparing you to fight or run, neither of which is particularly useful in a conference room.

And here's the kicker: that physiological response isn't even the main problem. The issue is what your mind *does* with it.

You feel your heart racing, and instead of recognizing it as a neutral physiological process, you interpret it as evidence. Evidence that you're about to fail. That everyone can see you're struggling. That you're not cut out for this. Your thoughts speed up, running simulations of potential disasters. You're not thinking about what you'll say next—you're already experiencing the imagined fallout from saying it wrong. The shame. The awkward silence. The subtle shift in how people perceive you.

This is anticipatory rumination, and it's a feedback loop from hell. The more you mentally rehearse potential failures, the more your body reacts as if they're happening *now*. Which gives you more physical symptoms to interpret as danger. Which fuels more catastrophic thinking. Round and round.

I'll tell you when I first noticed this pattern in myself, though I didn't have a name for it then. I was in my late twenties, leading a workshop on stress management—yes, the irony is not lost on me—and about twenty minutes before I was supposed to start, I locked myself in a bathroom stall. My hands were shaking. My mouth was dry. I'd facilitated dozens of these workshops. I knew the material cold. But in that moment, all I could think about was the facilitator evaluation forms participants would fill out afterward. What if my examples fell flat? What if someone asked a question I couldn't answer? What if they could *tell* I was anxious?

I remember gripping the toilet paper dispenser like it was the only solid thing in the world. My breathing had gone shallow and fast—that panicky rhythm where you're pulling air in but nothing seems to reach your lungs. I tried to talk myself down. "You've done this before. You know this stuff. Just breathe." But rational arguments don't work when your amygdala has decided you're in mortal danger. It's like trying to reason with a smoke alarm.

I gave the workshop. It went fine. People nodded in the right places, asked thoughtful questions, gave me decent scores. And I spent the entire ninety minutes in a state of heightened alert, scanning faces for signs of boredom or skepticism, mentally flagging every moment where I stumbled over a word or lost my train of thought.

Afterward, a colleague mentioned how calm and confident I'd seemed. I wanted to laugh. Or cry. I'd just burned through a week's worth of energy performing "calm and confident" while my nervous system treated the whole thing like a hostage negotiation.

That's the seduction of high-functioning anxiety in performance spaces. You *can* do it. You often do it well. So you assume the anxiety is manageable, maybe even useful. "I work best under pressure," you tell yourself. But pressure and panic aren't the same thing. And what you're calling pressure is often just free-floating dread that's learned to dress itself up as motivation.

The Real Cost of Performing While Your Nervous System Screams

The question isn't whether you can function while anxious. You've already proven you can. The question is: what's it costing you?

And I don't mean in some vague, metaphorical sense. I mean concretely. How much energy are you expending to maintain that performance? How present are you in the actual interaction versus the simulated version running in your head? How much of your life is spent in anticipatory dread of the next moment you'll be observed?

Let me paint you a picture of what this actually looks like.

You have a meeting scheduled for Thursday at two. On Monday, you notice the first flutter of dread. Just a whisper. A tightness in your chest when you think about it. You push it aside. You're busy. You have work to do.

Tuesday, the anxiety gets louder. You start mentally rehearsing what you'll say. Running through potential questions. Imagining how you'll respond. This feels productive—like preparation—but really you're just feeding the loop. Every scenario you run through is another opportunity for your brain to flag potential disasters.

By Wednesday night, you're not sleeping well. You wake up at three in the morning with your mind already spinning through the meeting. What if they ask about the thing you're not sure about? What if someone challenges your recommendation? What if you freeze?

Thursday morning, you can't eat. Your stomach is a knot. You change your outfit three times because nothing feels right—what you're really asking is "what will make me look most competent?" You arrive early. Too early. You sit in your car going through your notes one more time, even though you've already memorized them.

During the meeting itself, you're hypervigilant. Monitoring everyone's faces. Tracking who's engaged, who's checking their phone, who's frowning. When you speak, you hear your voice as if from outside yourself—is it shaking? Does it sound confident? Should you have phrased that differently? You make a small joke and it doesn't quite land and you feel the embarrassment flood through you, even though no one else seems to notice or care.

The meeting ends. It went fine. Actually, it went well. Your boss compliments your thoroughness. A colleague asks a follow-up question that suggests they found your ideas valuable.

And you spend the rest of the day—and probably the evening—replaying every moment. The joke that fell flat. The question you answered but maybe not as smoothly as you could have. The moment your mind went blank for half a second before you found the word you needed. Each tiny imperfection feels enormous in retrospect.

Friday, you're exhausted. Completely wrung out. You accomplished what you needed to accomplish, but it took everything you had.

That's the cost. Not just the ninety minutes of the meeting itself, but the four days of buildup and the aftermath. The sleep you lost. The energy you burned. The mental space that anxiety occupied when you could have been thinking about anything else. The way you were only half-present with your partner Wednesday night because part of you was still rehearsing for Thursday.

And here's the thing that really gets me: you probably didn't even count this as anxiety. You called it "preparing" or "being thorough" or "caring about doing well." The anxiety was so woven into your work process that you couldn't see it anymore. It was just how things got done.

This is what high-functioning anxiety actually costs. Not your performance—you're performing fine, maybe even better than fine. It costs your life. The parts of your life that aren't performing. The ability to be present. The capacity to rest. The energy you could be directing toward anything other than managing an internal threat-detection system that won't shut off.

You might be thinking, "Sure, but I *do* need to perform well. I can't just show up and wing it." And you're right. I'm not suggesting you abandon preparation or stop caring about outcomes. But there's a difference between wanting to do something well and treating every social interaction like a referendum on your worth as a person.

That's where things get complicated for people with high-functioning anxiety. We've tangled our performance with our identity so thoroughly that we can't separate them anymore. A slightly shaky voice isn't just a physiological response to adrenaline—it's evidence that we're weak. A momentary blank on someone's name isn't a normal memory lapse—it's proof we're socially incompetent. We've lost the ability to see these things as neutral data points and instead treat them as existential verdicts.

The Practice of Watching Yourself Without Dissolving

So what do you do with this? How do you show up to the things that matter without burning yourself out in the process?

Let me introduce you to what I call the Observer Practice, though I'll admit the name makes it sound more formal than it is. It's built on defusion techniques—creating distance between yourself and your internal experience—but with a specific focus on active witnessing rather than thought-stopping or suppression.

Here's how it works. When you notice yourself gearing up for a social situation—a presentation, a party, a difficult conversation—and you feel that familiar anxiety rising, you practice stepping back from it. Not suppressing it. Not reasoning with it. Just... observing it.

Imagine you're a researcher studying a subject. That subject happens to be you, but you're approaching it with curiosity rather than judgment. Notice the physical sensations without trying to change them. There's tightness in your chest—okay, that's interesting. Your pulse has quickened—noted. Your jaw is clenched—worth observing.

Then turn your attention to the thoughts. Not to argue with them or prove them wrong, but just to see them clearly. "I need to make a good impression." "They're going to notice if I stumble." "I can't afford to look incompetent."

Don't judge whether these thoughts are true or false. Don't try to replace them with positive affirmations. Just notice them as mental events—things your brain is producing, not facts about reality.

The crucial part—and this is where most people get tripped up—isn't making the anxiety go away. It's recognizing that sensations and thoughts are temporary. They arise, they peak, they pass. They don't define you. They don't control you, unless you grant them that power.

I know this sounds abstract. Let me give you a concrete example.

Marcus is a software architect in his mid-thirties. Technically brilliant. Consistently exceeds performance expectations. The kind of developer other developers go to when they're stuck on something complex. But he dreaded team meetings where he had to present his work. Not because he wasn't prepared—he over-prepared, if anything. But because the moment attention turned to him, his mind would flood with worst-case scenarios. What if he couldn't explain a technical decision clearly? What if someone pointed out a flaw in his approach? What if he froze mid-sentence?

The physical symptoms hit him hard. Days before a presentation, he'd notice tension creeping into his shoulders. His sleep would deteriorate—he'd lie awake running through his slides, anticipating questions. The morning of, his stomach would churn. He couldn't eat breakfast. He'd go through his slides obsessively, rehearsing every transition, anticipating every possible question, preparing answers for challenges that would probably never come.

The presentations themselves always went fine. He knew his material. He could answer technical questions in his sleep. But he'd stand there feeling like he was about to be exposed as a fraud, his heart hammering, his hands slightly trembling, hoping no one could see the sweat starting to form at his hairline.

When we started working together, I asked him to try something different. Instead of fighting the anxiety or trying to talk himself out of it, I wanted him to get curious about it.

The night before his next presentation, instead of drilling through his slides one more time, Marcus sat quietly and did a body scan. He noticed the tightness in his throat. The shallow quality of his breathing. The slight nausea. Instead of interpreting these as signs he wasn't ready, he simply named them. "Tight throat. Shallow breathing. Nausea." No judgment. Just observation.

Then he turned to his thoughts. "I'm going to forget something important. Someone's going to ask a question I can't answer. They'll think I don't know what I'm doing." He wrote them down, not to dispute them, but to see them on paper as discrete thoughts rather than overwhelming truths.

It felt strange to him at first. Almost performative, like he was pretending to be calm when he clearly wasn't. "This feels stupid," he told me later. "Like I'm just... narrating my anxiety instead of dealing with it."

But here's what started to shift: by observing the anxiety rather than being consumed by it, Marcus created a small gap between stimulus and response. The anxiety was still there—he could feel it, acknowledge it—but it wasn't running the show anymore.

During the presentation itself, when he felt his heart rate spike in response to a challenging question from the team lead, he paused. Not to gather his thoughts exactly, but to notice what was happening in his body. Feet on the floor. Hands on the table. Breath moving in and out. These sensations anchored him in the present moment, interrupting the catastrophic future-thinking that typically hijacked his attention.

He didn't suddenly become a polished public speaker. He still stumbled over a few words when explaining a particularly complex architectural decision. He didn't have a perfect answer to one of the questions about scalability and had to admit he'd need to think about it more and follow up.

But something fundamental had changed. Those imperfections didn't spiral him into shame. They were just... imperfections. Things that happen when humans talk to each other about complex topics. Not evidence of his inadequacy.

After the meeting, he didn't spend two hours replaying every moment. He noted that it had gone reasonably well, packed up his laptop, and moved on to his next task. That might sound small, but for Marcus, it was revolutionary. He'd reclaimed all that energy he usually spent in post-performance analysis.

Here's what I want you to understand: the Observer Practice isn't about achieving some zen state of perfect calm. It's about loosening anxiety's grip just enough that you can function *with* it rather than *despite* it. It's about recognizing that you can hold anxiety and still move forward.

Because here's the thing nobody tells you about high-functioning anxiety: it's not actually high-functioning at all. It's just anxiety that's learned to hide well.

Fast Tools for When Your Heart Is Trying to Escape Your Chest

Now let's get practical, because observation is one thing, but when you're standing in front of a room full of people and your heart is trying to punch its way out of your chest, you need tools that work *fast*.

Grounding techniques aren't distractions or tricks. They're ways of interrupting the feedback loop between your racing thoughts and your activated nervous system. They work by redirecting your attention from abstract worries to concrete, present-moment sensations. You're not fighting the anxiety. You're offering your brain something else to focus on—something real, something verifiable, something that isn't a threat.

One technique I return to again and again is what I call Five Things. It's almost embarrassingly simple, which is exactly why it works when your mind is spinning.

You pause—even for just a few seconds—and name five things you can see. Actually look at them. Notice the grain in the wooden table. The specific shade of blue on someone's shirt. The way light hits the window. Then name four things you can touch. Feel their texture. The smooth cool of your phone screen. The rough weave of the fabric on the chair. Three things you can hear. Maybe the hum of the ventilation system. Someone's voice in the hallway. The click of a keyboard. Two things you can smell. Even if it's just the coffee you had earlier or the faint scent of cleaning products. One thing you can taste. Maybe the mint from your gum or just the taste in your mouth.

This isn't meditation. It's not relaxation. It's sensory engagement. You're pulling your attention out of the future—where all the catastrophic thinking lives—and anchoring it in now. In this room. In this body.

I'll be honest: the first few times I tried this, I felt ridiculous. I was at a networking event—I hate networking events—feeling that familiar crawl of social anxiety, and I stood there mentally cataloging the things I could see while someone talked at me about their startup. The overhead lights (too bright, fluorescent). The conference center carpet (that particular pattern that exists only in conference centers and airports—burgundy and navy in some kind of geometric nightmare). The weight of the drink in my hand (gin and tonic, the ice already melting). The sound of dozens of conversations creating a low roar that made it hard to hear the person directly in front of me.

But it worked. Not completely. I was still uncomfortable. But the volume on the anxiety turned down just enough that I could actually hear what the person was saying instead of just waiting for my turn to perform. I caught myself actually getting interested in what they were building instead of monitoring my own facial expressions to make sure I looked interested.

Breathing techniques work on a similar principle, though they target the physiological response more directly. When you're anxious, your breathing typically becomes shallow and rapid—up in your chest instead of deep in your belly. This isn't just a symptom of anxiety—it actively maintains it. Shallow breathing signals to your nervous system that there's a threat, which keeps the stress response activated.

Box breathing is particularly effective because it's structured enough to occupy your attention but simple enough to remember under stress. Inhale for a count of four. Hold for four. Exhale for four. Hold for four. Repeat.

The counting gives your mind something to do—a task, a rhythm. The breath itself regulates your nervous system. But the real benefit is that you're taking back some agency over your physiological state. You're demonstrating to your nervous system that you're safe enough to breathe slowly.

Here's the thing, though: don't try to force your breathing into some perfect pattern. Don't try to *control* it with a clenched determination. That just creates another thing to be anxious about—"Am I breathing right? Is this working? What if I can't maintain the count?" Instead, observe your natural breath first. Notice its rhythm without judgment. Then gently guide it into a slower, deeper pattern. If you lose count, that's fine. Start over. If your breath wants to quicken again, let it, then guide it back.

Let me tell you about Rachel, a marketing director who volunteered for high-stakes presentations despite knowing each one would trigger significant anxiety. Actually, "volunteered" isn't quite right—she specifically sought them out. She believed—and this is common—that the anxiety meant she cared about doing well. That it kept her sharp. That without it, she'd get complacent and her work would suffer.

Before a recent pitch to a major potential client—a retail chain that could triple her company's revenue if they signed—she felt the familiar tightness building in her chest as she waited for her turn to present. Palms sweating. Mind racing through everything that could go wrong. She'd practiced extensively. Her slides were perfect. She'd rehearsed her delivery until she could do it in her sleep. None of that mattered to her nervous system, which was convinced she was about to be publicly humiliated.

The CEO was presenting first, walking through the company overview. Rachel sat at the conference table, gripping her pen too tightly, barely hearing what he was saying. In her peripheral vision, she could see the clients—three executives whose expressions gave away nothing. Were they interested? Skeptical? Already decided this was a waste of time?

Instead of trying to suppress the anxiety—which had never worked anyway—she shifted her focus. While her colleague presented, Rachel subtly began Five Things. The warm overhead lights casting a slight yellow glow. The texture of the chair fabric against her legs—that commercial-grade upholstery that's designed to last forever but not to be comfortable. The muted carpet pattern, similar to the one from that networking event. The dark conference table, polished enough that she could see a blurred reflection. The silver clasp on her colleague's bracelet, catching the light when she gestured.

Nothing dramatic. Just observation. The anxiety didn't vanish—it never does—but its intensity dropped just enough for her to breathe.

When she stood to present, she incorporated box breathing. Not obviously—no exaggerated inhales that would make people wonder what was wrong. Just a quiet internal rhythm. Inhale, two, three, four. Hold, two, three, four. Exhale, two, three, four. Hold, two, three, four.

She could feel her shoulders beginning to release. The tightness in her chest easing slightly. She made eye contact with one of the executives—a woman in her fifties with glasses and an expression Rachel couldn't quite read—and instead of immediately spiraling into "does she look bored? Can she tell I'm nervous? Did I already lose her?"—Rachel just... looked back. Human to human. Then moved on.

Midway through, she stumbled over a sentence while explaining their proposed timeline. Just a small verbal slip—she said "we'll deliver the initial analytics in two, in three weeks" before correcting herself. In the past, that would've been catastrophic. Proof that she was failing. That everyone could see through her. That she shouldn't be doing this. The embarrassment would have flooded through her, disrupting her flow, making her rush through the rest to get it over with.

This time, she took a breath. Corrected herself. Kept going.

The anxiety didn't disappear. It hummed beneath the surface the entire time, a constant low-level alert. But she'd created enough space around it—enough regulation—that she could function. Not despite the anxiety, but alongside it.

They won the contract. But what struck Rachel more than the win was the energy she had afterward. Usually, successful presentations left her completely depleted—she'd need to go home and collapse, wrung out from the internal battle. This time, she was tired but not destroyed. She actually had the bandwidth to celebrate with her team instead of needing to retreat and recover.

Midway through, she stumbled over a sentence while explaining their proposed timeline. "Just a small verbal slip," she said. "We'll deliver the initial analysis in two to three weeks," before correcting herself. In the past, that would've been an airtight sign that she was failing. That everyone could see through her. [illegible] doing this. The embarrassment would have flooded through her, [illegible] her [illegible] through the rest [illegible] with.

The [illegible] could [illegible] herself. [illegible]

The [illegible] murmured beneath the surface the [illegible] [illegible]

[illegible]

was the [illegible] and [illegible] left [illegible] [illegible]

Why Eliminating Anxiety Is the Wrong Goal

You might be wondering why I keep emphasizing that these techniques don't eliminate anxiety. Why not aim higher? Why not try to eradicate it completely?

Because that's not how humans work. Anxiety is a normal response to uncertainty, to novelty, to situations where we're being evaluated. The goal isn't to become some emotionless robot who glides through social situations without a care. The goal is to change your relationship to the discomfort. To stop treating it as a problem to be solved and start recognizing it as information—sometimes useful, often overblown, always temporary.

When you set elimination as the goal, you're actually setting yourself up for more suffering. Because now you have the original anxiety *plus* anxiety about the anxiety. "Why am I still anxious? I tried the breathing. I did the grounding. What's wrong with me? Why can't I just be calm?"

That's not regulation. That's just another form of the performance trap—trying to perform "being calm" while judging yourself for not achieving it perfectly.

Here's what actually helps: accepting that some level of activation is normal and expected when you're doing something that matters to you. The issue isn't the presence of anxiety. It's the volume. It's whether the anxiety is proportionate to the actual situation. It's whether you can still access your skills and presence while it's happening.

Think about athletes before a big game. Their heart rate is elevated. Their nervous system is activated. They're experiencing what we'd call anxiety in any other context. But they've learned to interpret that activation as readiness, not threat. The physiological state is the same—it's the relationship to it that differs.

The Invisible Rules That Keep You Trapped

What really keeps us stuck in social anxiety isn't the physiological response itself. It's the rigid, unspoken rules we've internalized about how we're supposed to behave. These aren't conscious beliefs exactly. They're more like operating assumptions that run in the background, dictating our every move.

Eye contact must be maintained for a specific duration—not too little, which signals dishonesty or disinterest, and not too much, which is aggressive or weird. You've probably never articulated this rule explicitly, but try violating it and see what happens. The discomfort rises immediately.

Jokes need to land perfectly or they shouldn't be told at all. Any humor that falls flat is a failure that will be remembered and cataloged against you.

Silences are emergencies that must be filled immediately. If a conversation lulls, it's your responsibility to rescue it, and failing to do so means you're socially incompetent.

Any display of uncertainty is weakness. You should always project confidence, even when you're unsure. Admitting you don't know something is professional suicide.

Any admission of anxiety is doubly damning—not only are you anxious, but you've also revealed it, which proves you can't handle the pressure.

These rules are exhausting. And completely unrealistic.

But here's the insidious part: they feel true. They feel like objective facts about how social situations work, not arbitrary standards you've internalized. So you don't question them. You just keep trying to follow them, and when you inevitably fail—because no human can maintain that level of controlled performance—you interpret it as a personal deficiency.

What's actually happening when you try to follow these rules? Your nervous system interprets every deviation—every awkward pause, every moment of less-than-perfect eye contact—as a failure. The amygdala fires. Cortisol and adrenaline flood your system. You're not just having a conversation. You're performing, constantly monitoring yourself, adjusting, course-correcting, trying desperately to hit some invisible standard of acceptable social behavior.

And the cruelest part? All this self-monitoring makes you *less* present, not more. You're so focused on how you're being perceived that you can't actually engage with what's happening. You miss half of what people say because you're too busy tracking your own performance. You can't connect authentically because you're following a script written by anxiety.

Practicing the Art of Good Enough

The regulation tool here isn't suppression. It's intentional imperfection. It's deliberately loosening your grip on control and experimenting with what happens when you let yourself be less than perfect.

This sounds terrifying, I know. When I first suggested this to clients, they'd look at me like I'd asked them to juggle knives while blindfolded. "You want me to deliberately be awkward? To let things go wrong?" Not exactly. I want you to test whether the consequences you fear are actually real.

Start small. Allow yourself a brief moment of eye aversion during a conversation—look away to think, to process, because that's what humans actually do. Share a self-deprecating story where you're not the hero. Admit you don't know something instead of bluffing your way through. Let a silence sit for a few seconds without rushing to fill it.

The goal isn't to be deliberately awkward—it's to demonstrate to yourself that you can survive, even thrive, when things aren't perfectly controlled. That most of those rigid rules you're following aren't actually necessary. That people are far more forgiving and less attentive to your minor imperfections than your anxiety insists.

It's practicing the art of good enough.

Maya was a project manager known for being meticulous and polished. Socially, though, she felt like she was constantly on the edge of disaster. She'd plan dinner parties down to the smallest detail—the menu, the seating arrangement, backup topics of conversation in case things lagged. She'd rehearse interactions in advance. Map out potential conversational branches. But inevitably, something would go "wrong"—a comment that landed awkwardly, a silence she couldn't fill, someone's expression she interpreted as judgment. And she'd spend hours afterward dissecting the interaction, convinced she'd ruined everything.

The dinner parties themselves were lovely. Her friends enjoyed them. They told her so. But Maya couldn't hear it. She was too busy cataloging her failures.

We started by identifying the unspoken rules she was operating under. "I must always appear competent and in control." "I should be able to steer every conversation smoothly." "Any vulnerability is weakness." "If people see me struggling, they'll lose respect for me."

Then we practiced breaking them. In small, controlled ways at first.

During our sessions, I'd ask her to deliberately stumble over a sentence. To admit she didn't know something. To let a silence sit without rushing to fill it. These exercises felt excruciating to her at first. Every instinct screamed at her to fix it, to smooth it over, to perform competence.

But gradually, something shifted. She started to notice that the world didn't end when she let a sentence trail off. That people didn't judge her harshly when she said "I don't know." That silences weren't emergencies—sometimes they were just... pauses. Natural rhythms in conversation.

She tried it in her real life. At a work meeting, when someone asked about a technical detail she wasn't sure about, instead of offering a vague non-answer that protected her image, she said, "That's a good question. I'd need to check the documentation to give you an accurate answer."

The world didn't end. Her colleague nodded, made a note, and the conversation moved on. No one seemed to think less of her. In fact, someone else chimed in with their own uncertainty about a related issue, and suddenly the meeting became a collaborative problem-solving session instead of a performance where everyone pretended to have all the answers.

At her next dinner party, when a conversational lull happened—that natural dip that occurs when people are eating, or thinking, or just comfortable enough not to fill every second with sound—Maya didn't panic. She let it sit. Sipped her wine. And after a few seconds, one of her friends launched into a story about something that had happened to them that week.

The silence hadn't needed rescuing. It had just been a breath.

What Social Anxiety Actually Protects You From (and What It Costs)

Here's what I've come to understand about social anxiety after years of working with it, both professionally and in myself: it's not irrational. It's not a malfunction. It's a protection system that's working exactly as designed—it's just protecting you from the wrong thing.

What does social anxiety protect you from? The feeling of vulnerability. The exposure of being seen, really seen, in your uncertainty or imperfection. The potential for rejection or judgment.

These are not trivial threats. We're social creatures. Being rejected by our community, historically, could mean death. Your nervous system isn't being dramatic when it treats social threat as serious. It's doing its job.

But here's what it costs you: connection. Presence. The ability to be yourself instead of a carefully managed version of yourself. The energy you could be directing toward actually engaging with people instead of monitoring how you're being perceived.

Think about the last time you had a conversation that felt effortless. Where you weren't tracking your performance, weren't worried about how you were coming across, weren't rehearsing your next response while the other person was still talking. Chances are, it was with someone you felt completely safe with—maybe a close friend, maybe a sibling, maybe a partner. Someone whose judgment you didn't fear.

What did that feel like? Probably lighter. Easier. Maybe even energizing instead of draining.

That's what's available when you're not running the anxiety program in the background. Not all the time—probably not even most of the time, at least not at first. But more than you currently experience.

The regulation work isn't about eliminating the protection system. It's about updating its threat assessment. Teaching it that most social situations aren't actually life-or-death. That minor imperfections won't lead to catastrophic rejection. That you can handle discomfort without dissolving.

The Exposure That Actually Works

Traditional exposure therapy for social anxiety often looks like this: identify the thing you fear, then force yourself to do it repeatedly until the fear diminishes. Fear public speaking? Give lots of speeches. Anxious in groups? Attend more social events.

And sometimes that works. Repeated exposure can reduce the fear response over time. But it can also backfire spectacularly if you're just white-knuckling through the experience, proving to yourself over and over that social situations are indeed terrible.

What works better—what actually creates lasting change—is exposure plus processing. You put yourself in the situation, yes, but you also practice a different relationship to the discomfort that arises.

This means deliberately noticing your anxiety without judging it. Experimenting with small imperfections. Staying present instead of dissociating into performance mode. And afterward—and this is crucial—reflecting on what actually happened versus what you feared would happen.

That gap between expectation and reality is where the learning happens.

I worked with a client named David who had intense anxiety around speaking in meetings. He'd attend, but he'd rarely contribute unless directly asked. And when he did speak, he'd feel his face flush, his voice shake slightly, his thoughts scatter. Afterward, he'd replay the moment obsessively, convinced everyone had noticed his anxiety and judged him for it.

We started with small experiments. In his next meeting, David committed to making one comment—just one. Not a major contribution. Not something that required him to speak for minutes. Just a single relevant observation.

Before the meeting, he did the Observer Practice. Noticed the anxiety. Named the physical sensations. Acknowledged the thoughts without arguing with them.

During the meeting, when he felt the impulse to contribute, he used box breathing. Four counts in. Four counts hold. Four counts out. Four counts hold. Then he spoke.

His voice did shake slightly. He noticed it but didn't stop talking. He made his point—something about the timeline on a project—and then stopped. Resisted the urge to fill the silence with additional explanation or justification.

One of his colleagues nodded and said, "Good point, we should factor that in." The conversation moved on.

Afterward, David's instinct was to replay the moment, cataloging everything that had gone wrong. The shakiness in his voice. The slight stumble over a word. But instead, he pulled out his phone and made a note of what had actually happened.

What he'd feared: That he'd be so anxious he wouldn't be able to speak coherently. That people would notice his anxiety and think he was incompetent. That he'd say something stupid and people would judge him. That his voice would shake so badly he'd have to stop mid-sentence.

What actually happened: He spoke. His voice shook slightly, but not enough to derail him. He made a relevant point. A colleague agreed with him. The meeting continued.

That gap—between the catastrophe he'd imagined and the mundane reality of what occurred—that's the information his nervous system needed. Not intellectual understanding that "it'll be fine." Experiential evidence that he could feel anxious and still function. That minor imperfections weren't catastrophic.

Over time, David increased his contributions. Not every meeting—some days the anxiety was too high and he honored that. But more often than before. And each time, he collected more evidence that his fears were disproportionate to reality.

The anxiety didn't disappear. But its volume decreased. And his willingness to act despite it increased.

When the Anxiety Is Telling You Something Real

I need to add a caveat here, because I don't want to suggest that all social anxiety is just irrational fear that needs to be overcome.

Sometimes, your anxiety is picking up on something real. Sometimes the environment actually isn't safe. Sometimes the people you're with are actually judgmental, or the power dynamics are actually threatening, or the situation genuinely requires a level of performance you're not prepared for.

I've watched people with social anxiety push themselves into situations that their gut was telling them to avoid, labeling that gut feeling as "just anxiety" when it was actually wisdom.

There's a difference between anxiety that's protective and anxiety that's overprotective. The first alerts you to genuine mismatches or threats. The second treats every social situation like a potential disaster.

Learning to distinguish between them is part of the work.

Here's a useful question: Is this anxiety proportionate to the actual situation? If you're anxious about giving a presentation to your small team on a topic you know well, that's likely overprotection. Your nervous system is treating a low-stakes situation as high-stakes. If you're anxious about confronting someone who has a history of aggressive responses, that's probably protective. Your nervous system is picking up on real danger.

Another question: Does this anxiety improve with exposure, or does it get worse? If you've attended the same weekly team meeting for months and you're still as anxious as you were the first time, that might be a signal that something about the environment isn't working for you. Maybe it's the way meetings are run. Maybe it's a specific person's behavior. Maybe it's a culture that doesn't align with your values.

Regulation tools can help you function in difficult environments. But they're not meant to make you tolerate genuinely harmful situations indefinitely.

Part of managing anxiety in performance spaces is knowing when to regulate and when to extract yourself.

Building Your Own Protocol

Here's what I want you to take from this chapter, not as abstract theory but as something you can actually use:

Before your next situation that typically triggers social anxiety—whatever that is for you—try this protocol.

Before: Do the Observer Practice. Scan your body. Notice where you're holding tension. Name the physical sensations without trying to change them. Notice your thoughts. Write them down if that helps. Don't argue with them. Just acknowledge them as mental events, not facts.

During: Use Five Things if you feel the anxiety spiking. Name what you can see, touch, hear, smell, taste. Use box breathing to regulate your nervous system. Four counts in, four counts hold, four counts out, four counts hold. Don't aim for perfection. Just aim for presence.

Experiment with one intentional imperfection. Let a silence sit. Admit you don't know something. Allow your voice to shake without stopping. Break one of your rigid rules and observe what happens.

After: Don't replay the moment looking for failures. Instead, note the gap between what you feared and what actually happened. Write it down. That gap is data your nervous system needs.

What you feared:

What actually happened:

Do this enough times and you start to recalibrate. The anxiety doesn't vanish—I keep saying this because it's important—but it stops running the show. You start to trust that you can feel uncomfortable and still function. That imperfection isn't catastrophe. That you're more resilient than your anxiety gives you credit for.

And maybe, eventually, you start to show up to social situations not as a performance to be executed but as a human being who's allowed to be uncertain, imperfect, and real. Which, it turns out, is what actual connection requires anyway.

Chapter 8: From Suppression to Expression

I watched a video once of Simone Biles withdrawing from the Tokyo Olympics. Not the announcement—the moments before. The footage shows her sitting alone, wrapped in a towel, staring at nothing. Her teammates are stretching, preparing. She's perfectly still. What struck me wasn't the decision itself, but how long she'd been holding it together before that moment. Days of competing while something fundamental had broken in her proprioception—that internal sense of where your body is in space. She called it "the twisties." Gymnasts know it as the thing that can kill you: your mind and body suddenly, catastrophically out of sync mid-flight.

I keep coming back to that image because it captures something most of us with high-functioning anxiety live with constantly, just at a lower altitude. We're not flipping through the air, but we are perpetually mid-performance. And we're very, very good at staying still and silent while something inside us is screaming.

Three weeks ago, I sat at my sister's dining table for what should have been an ordinary Sunday dinner. Roast chicken. Green beans. Her kids arguing over who got the drumstick. Normal. My sister passed me the potatoes and paused, her hand still on the bowl. "Are you okay?" she asked. "You seem tense."

"I'm great!" I said. Smiled. Took the potatoes.

The truth: my jaw was clenched so tight I could barely chew. I'd been grinding my teeth through the entire meal without noticing—my body screaming while I performed ease. I realized it only because she said something, and even then my first instinct was to deny it. To smooth it over. To prove I was fine.

Later that night I found myself in the bathroom pressing my fingers into the hinge of my jaw, trying to release the knot of muscle there. When did that happen? How long had I been doing that? The scary part wasn't the tension itself—it was that I'd completely lost access to the signal. My body had been trying to tell me something for probably an hour, maybe longer, and I'd overridden it so completely I didn't even register the pain until someone else noticed it in my face.

This is what chronic suppression does. It doesn't make the feeling go away. It just trains you to stop hearing the alarm.

If you live with high-functioning anxiety, you've probably experienced this: You're scrolling through your calendar and spot an event three weeks out. A work conference. A presentation. Maybe just dinner with people you don't know well. And before you've even begun to prepare, your chest tightens. Your stomach clenches. Suddenly you're not thinking about what will *likely* happen—you're cataloging everything that could go wrong. You'll stumble over your words. You'll forget someone's name. You'll say something awkward and everyone will notice and you'll replay it for months afterward.

You haven't even started preparing, and you're already exhausted.

This isn't fear of failure, exactly. It's fear of being unmasked. Of the carefully constructed facade slipping just enough that people see what's underneath—the doubt, the effort, the sheer amount of energy it takes to appear this competent.

Here's what's happening in your body during that moment: Your amygdala—the brain's threat-detection center—can't distinguish between a present danger and a potential one three weeks away. It scans for anything that deviates from safety, from predictability. And because you've likely spent years training yourself to perceive any loss of control as dangerous, even a routine work event can trigger a full threat response.

Now here's where it gets complicated. You've developed strategies for managing this. Deep breathing. Meticulous planning. Mental rehearsal. Physical tension to "hold it together." These aren't bad strategies. They help you function. They help you achieve. But when they become automatic—when you consistently override your emotional responses before they fully register—something shifts.

Think of emotions as energy seeking expression. They're signals designed to move through you and prompt action. When you suppress that energy instead of letting it flow, you're not making it disappear. You're forcing it inward. The muscles stay tense. The breath stays shallow. Cortisol circulates. And it accumulates.

I used to think this was just about psychology—about thoughts and feelings and cognitive patterns. Then I started paying attention to the physical toll. Chronic muscle tension creates headaches, neck pain, back problems that seem to come from nowhere. Shallow breathing restricts oxygen, leaving you foggy and depleted even after a full night's sleep. Sustained cortisol exposure weakens your immune system (I got sick constantly for two years and kept blaming it on bad luck). It disrupts digestion—hence the knot in your stomach that appears every time something stressful is on the horizon.

The body isn't designed for sustained low-grade stress. It's built for acute bursts—a threat appears, you respond, it resolves, you rest. But when you're perpetually in threat-response mode, when rest never comes because you never fully allow the discharge, the system breaks down.

And here's the truly insidious part: Emotional suppression actually *increases* anxiety over time. By repeatedly telling yourself not to feel, you create a feedback loop where even mild discomfort feels overwhelming. Your nervous system becomes hypervigilant, constantly scanning for threats, because it's learned that any expression of vulnerability is itself dangerous. You're tightening a knot every time you try to loosen it.

So what's the alternative?

It's not about unleashing every feeling without filter. That's neither sustainable nor helpful. And it's definitely not about letting anxiety dictate your choices.

It's about allowing yourself to *feel* without judgment—to acknowledge what's happening inside you without immediately trying to fix it or make it go away.

Let me give you something practical, something you can try today: the Emotional Weather Report.

Three or four times throughout the day, pause for thirty seconds. Don't analyze. Don't problem-solve. Just notice what sensations are present. Is your chest tight? Shoulders tense? Stomach knotted? Then assign it a weather descriptor: sunny, cloudy, drizzly, stormy.

The key—and this is harder than it sounds—is to avoid labeling it as "anxiety" or framing it as something wrong. You're just observing. You're checking the internal weather without getting swept up in it.

I know how this sounds. It sounds too simple to matter. But here's why it works: Most of us with high-functioning anxiety have spent so long suppressing our internal experience that we've lost the ability to simply *notice* without immediately moving to intervention. We feel tension, and instantly we're strategizing how to eliminate it. We skip right over the acknowledgment phase.

The weather report creates a tiny gap between sensation and reaction. And in that gap, something shifts.

Let me tell you about Elena Ferrante. Not the writer—a different Elena, a litigation attorney I spoke with last year who'd been referred to me by her doctor. She was having what her cardiologist had ruled out as heart problems: chest tightness, racing pulse, occasional sharp pains that left her convinced she was dying. Every test came back normal. "It's anxiety," they told her. She didn't believe them.

Elena prepared for trials the way a lot of high-achievers prepare for high-stakes events: obsessively. The week before a major case, she'd work sixteen-hour days, refining arguments, anticipating every possible objection, memorizing case law. She'd script potential cross-examinations in her head while lying awake at 3 AM. She told herself this was just part of being good at her job. And she *was* good—she won most of her cases.

But her body was keeping score.

When we started working together, I asked her to try the weather report—just notice, throughout the week leading up to her next trial, what sensations appeared and when. No intervention, no fixing. Just data collection.

Monday morning, reviewing case files: tightness in her jaw, tension across her shoulders. Partly cloudy.

Tuesday afternoon, drafting her opening statement: knot in her stomach, shallow breathing. Overcast.

Wednesday evening, running through cross-examination scenarios: heart racing, hands trembling slightly. Storm building.

She didn't try to change any of it. She just noted it. And here's what she discovered: The sensations weren't constant. They came in waves. The tight chest would peak and then, if she didn't resist it, it would start to ease on its own. The knot in her stomach would shift, loosen slightly, sometimes disappear entirely for hours before returning.

By Friday, she noticed something else: Her attempts to *control* the anxiety—the extra hours of preparation, the mental rehearsal, the sheer force of will—were actually intensifying it. The more she tried to eliminate uncertainty, the more her body interpreted the situation as genuinely dangerous.

The trial went fine. Not perfect—she stumbled over a witness's name, forgot a reference she'd planned to include—but fine. What changed wasn't the anxiety. She still felt it. What changed was her relationship to it.

She'd spent years treating anxiety as evidence that something was wrong, that she wasn't prepared enough, that catastrophe was imminent. But once she started simply observing it as weather—something passing through rather than something she needed to battle—it lost some of its power.

Here's what I wish someone had told me years ago: Feeling anxious doesn't mean you're incompetent. It means you're human, navigating something that matters to you.

The goal isn't to become fearless. The goal is to expand your capacity to hold discomfort without falling apart.

Think about that phrasing for a second: "hold discomfort." Not eliminate it. Not fix it. Not overcome it. Just... hold it. Like you'd hold a hot cup of coffee—carefully, with awareness, knowing it won't stay this hot forever.

This is the shift from suppression to expression. Not expression as in emotional outburst. Expression as in allowing the energy to move through you instead of damming it up inside.

So what does that actually look like?

For some people, it's journaling. And I don't mean the kind of journaling where you produce beautiful, coherent prose about your feelings. I mean the kind where you dump whatever's in your head onto the page without editing, without censoring, without worrying if it makes sense. It's opening a pressure valve.

For others—especially those of us with high-functioning anxiety who find that kind of freeform approach overwhelming—structure helps. Writing in response to specific prompts. "What does this anxiety feel like in my body?" "If this feeling could speak, what would it say?" "What am I actually afraid will happen?"

I've found that the process matters more than the product. You're not trying to solve anything or gain insight (though that sometimes happens). You're creating a private space where you don't have to perform. Where you can be messy and uncertain and afraid without consequence.

Creative outlets work the same way. Painting, music, movement—anything that lets you channel internal experience into external form. It doesn't matter if you're "good" at it. That's not the point. The point is that you're giving the energy somewhere to go.

I started drawing a few years ago. Terrible drawings, genuinely. But when I'm feeling that tight, wound-up sensation and I can't quite name what's wrong, I'll sit with a sketchbook and just... make marks. Scribbles, shapes, color. It bypasses the part of my brain that wants to analyze and fix everything. And afterward, I usually feel lighter. Not because I've solved anything, but because I've let something out.

Talking to someone you trust is another essential piece. Not to get advice or solutions, but just to be heard. To say out loud, "I'm struggling with this," and have someone respond with something other than "Have you tried not worrying about it?"

Finding the right person matters. Someone who won't judge or minimize your experience. Someone who can hold space for your vulnerability without trying to fix it or make it go away.

For me, that person is my friend Marcus. We've known each other since college, and somewhere along the way we developed this unspoken agreement: When one of us is in it—really in it—the other just listens. No advice unless asked. No "everything happens for a reason" platitudes. Just: "That sounds really hard. I'm here."

I can't overstate how much that matters. How rare it is to be allowed to feel difficult things without someone immediately trying to solve them.

Therapy can offer that too, if you find the right therapist. A place where you're not expected to be the competent, capable version of yourself. Where you can be uncertain and afraid and imperfect.

Let me tell you what happened with Liam.

Liam ran a small architecture firm. Successful, respected, perpetually tense. His wife described him as "distant"—not in a cruel way, just accurate. She rarely saw him not working. When they talked about it, he'd acknowledge that he felt irritable. A low-grade frustration that seemed to cling to him. But he'd rationalized it for years: deadline stress, not enough sleep, normal stuff everyone deals with.

It wasn't anxiety. Not the way people usually described it.

What was actually happening: Liam had learned early that expressing anger or sadness was unprofessional. His father—a stoic engineer—had modeled emotional restraint as virtue. Vulnerability equaled failure. So Liam developed a physical holding pattern: chronic jaw tension, tight shoulders, shallow breath, constant internal monitoring for any emotion he deemed unacceptable.

He wasn't avoiding feeling. He was subtly, relentlessly squeezing it down, redirecting the energy into productivity.

It worked, in a way. He was incredibly efficient. But it depleted him. It eroded his relationship with his wife. And it left him feeling perpetually disconnected—from himself, from other people, from any sense of ease.

We started with guided imagery exercises—visualization practices to help him connect with his body and identify where he was holding tension. It felt awkward at first. He was used to *doing*, not *feeling*. But gradually he began noticing the signals: the tightness in his chest when a client's request felt unreasonable, the jaw clench when his wife expressed disappointment.

Then we tried expressive writing. Not journaling about daily events, but responding to prompts like "What does anger feel like in your body?" or "If sadness could speak, what would it say?"

He resisted. It felt unproductive. Indulgent, even.

But I framed it as an experiment—data collection about his internal experience. He started small. Five minutes a day. And slowly, he began articulating emotions he'd been suppressing for years: frustration with demanding clients, sadness about a strained relationship with his brother, fear of not meeting expectations.

There were no dramatic breakthroughs. No cathartic crying sessions. Just a slow crack in the wall.

He started incorporating small acts of self-compassion into his routine. Taking deep breaths when overwhelmed without telling himself he should already be past this. Allowing breaks without guilt. Acknowledging his accomplishments, even small ones.

And he started sharing some of this with his wife. Tentatively at first. Instead of presenting a polished exterior, he'd admit when he was struggling, when he needed support.

It wasn't easy. Years of conditioning don't vanish overnight. But their connection deepened. The irritability didn't disappear, but it no longer clung to him with the same intensity. He discovered that acknowledging his feelings gave him more control over them, not less. It let him respond thoughtfully instead of react impulsively.

And the work changed too. More creative solutions. Better collaboration. Greater fulfillment. The architecture hadn't changed. But he had.

There's a crucial distinction I need to make here, because it gets blurred a lot in conversations about emotional health: Allowing yourself to feel is not the same as letting feelings dictate your actions.

We're not aiming for unrestrained outpouring. We're aiming for regulated expression.

Think of it like an engine with release valves. The valves prevent overheating, but they don't just open randomly. They respond to pressure, releasing energy in a controlled way.

Acknowledging your feelings isn't about abandoning boundaries or becoming unpredictable. It's about recognizing the internal build-up, understanding what's driving it, and then choosing how—and when and where—to let some of that pressure out.

The trouble with high-functioning anxiety is that we become incredibly skilled at managing outward appearances. We perform competence. But the energy doesn't disappear. It gets rerouted into physiological tension, digestive issues, chronic pain, the relentless mental checklist. It becomes part of the invisible load we carry.

And when we finally do crack, it's rarely a graceful release. It's an explosion born from months or years of accumulated pressure.

I think about Amelia.

She was a project manager, known for being unflappable. Deadlines loomed? No problem. Crisis hit? She stayed calm, implemented solutions, moved on. But behind the scenes, she felt like a tightly wound spring.

When people asked how she was doing, she'd say some version of "Fine, just busy." Not because she was lying—she simply hadn't practiced accessing or articulating her internal experience.

The breaking point came during a demanding product launch. A critical bug surfaced late in the process, and Amelia—instead of delegating or asking for help, strategies she routinely encouraged her team to use—tried to fix it herself. She worked through the night. The code wouldn't cooperate. Hours blurred. At 3 AM, she started weeping. Not dramatic crying, just... couldn't stop.

Her team found her that way, convinced something catastrophic had happened with the project.

But nothing catastrophic had happened with the project. The bug was fixable. What had happened was system overload. Years of suppressing discomfort—the anxiety around potential failure, the pressure to appear perfect, the fear of disappointing people—had created a pressure cooker. The bug was just the trigger.

Afterward, she felt immense shame. She was certain her team had lost respect for her.

But when we unpacked what happened *before* the tears, we found something important: She hadn't registered the escalating tension until it was too late. She'd bypassed all the early signals—the knot in her stomach, the tightness in her shoulders, the shallow breathing—and gone straight to catastrophic failure.

We started simple: body scans throughout the day. Three minutes, several times daily. Just checking in with physical sensations without judgment. Where are you holding tension? What does it feel like? Is your breath shallow or deep?

Not trying to fix anything. Just noticing.

Then came the harder part: translating internal signals into language. Instead of automatically saying "I'm fine," we practiced other responses. "I'm feeling a little overwhelmed right now." "I'm stressed about this deadline." "I'm worried I'm going to mess this up."

Simple statements. But for Amelia, who'd spent her entire professional life projecting competence, they felt terrifying. Like admitting weakness. Like inviting judgment.

Here's what actually happened when she started saying these things: Her team didn't lose respect for her. They felt closer to her. They started sharing their own struggles more openly. The culture shifted—became more honest, more collaborative, less performative.

And Amelia learned that she could acknowledge difficulty without falling apart. That naming what she was feeling actually gave her more agency, not less.

Let me be clear about something: This work isn't about indulging in negativity or wallowing in difficult emotions. It's not about making anxiety the center of your identity or using it as an excuse.

It's about acknowledging the full spectrum of human experience—joy, sorrow, anger, fear—and recognizing that each has its place. That suppressing them doesn't make them disappear. It drives them underground, where they fester and manifest in ways that are actually harder to manage.

I think we're taught, especially those of us who are high-achieving, that emotional control equals strength. That the goal is to transcend feelings, to operate purely from logic and willpower.

But that's not how humans work. We're not computers. Emotions aren't bugs in the system—they're features. They provide information. They connect us to ourselves and to other people. They make life textured and meaningful instead of just a series of tasks to complete.

The real strength isn't in eliminating emotion. It's in developing the capacity to feel deeply without being controlled by those feelings. To let fear exist without letting it make your decisions. To acknowledge sadness without letting it define you. To experience anger without lashing out.

That capacity—that ability to hold the full range of your experience with compassion and without judgment—is what actually allows you to thrive. Not the performance of having it all together. Not the facade of fearlessness.

Just the willingness to be human. To be imperfect. To sometimes struggle, and to let that be okay.

I started this chapter with Simone Biles sitting alone in that towel, wrapped in stillness while everything inside her was out of sync. I think about her a lot when I'm working with people who have high-functioning anxiety, because she did something most of us find almost impossible: She stopped performing.

In front of the entire world, with unimaginable pressure, she said, "Something is wrong and I can't ignore it anymore."

That's not failure. That's courage.

Most of us aren't operating at that level of visibility. We're not Olympic athletes with millions watching. But we are performing, constantly, for an audience of colleagues and family and friends and—most demandingly—ourselves.

And what I want you to consider is this: What would it feel like to stop performing, even just for a moment? To let someone see you struggling? To admit that you're not fine, that you're carrying more than you can comfortably hold?

Not because you want to be rescued. Not because you need someone to fix it. Just because it's true.

Because here's what I've learned, both from my own experience and from watching other people navigate this: The performance is exhausting. It takes enormous energy to maintain that facade. Energy you could be using for things that actually matter to you.

And the irony is that the people around you—the ones you're performing for—mostly don't need you to be perfect. They need you to be real. They're probably performing for you too, waiting for permission to be honest about their own struggles.

What if you gave them that permission by going first?

What if, the next time someone asks if you're okay, you told them the truth?

Not the performative truth. Not "I'm great!" while your jaw is clenched so tight you can barely chew. But the real truth: "Actually, I'm really anxious about this thing and I'm not sure how to handle it."

You might be surprised by what happens next. Not always—some people won't know what to do with that honesty. But often enough, you'll find that the vulnerability you offer creates space for someone else to be vulnerable too.

And in that space, something shifts. The isolation eases. The performance drops. You remember that you're not alone in this, that struggle is part of being human, not evidence that you're doing it wrong.

You remember that the goal was never to be fearless. It was to be brave enough to feel the fear and move forward anyway. To let yourself be seen—really seen—and discover that you're still worthy of love and belonging even when you're not holding it all together.

That's the work. Not becoming perfect at managing anxiety. Not eliminating discomfort. Just learning to meet yourself with the same compassion you'd offer someone you love. Just building the capacity to hold your own experience, whatever it is, without judgment.

Just finding your way back to being human, instead of the polished performance of what you think human should look like.

The next time your chest tightens three weeks before an event, or your sister asks if you're okay at dinner, or you find yourself at 3 AM unable to let go of something that went wrong—what if you just let it be there? What if you named it, acknowledged it, maybe even told someone about it?

What if the very thing you've been trying so hard to control is actually the doorway to something you've been looking for all along?

Chapter 9: Sustaining Regulation Long-Term

I kept a list once. Started sometime in March 2019—not because a therapist told me to, but because I'd wake up at 2 AM with my heart hammering and no idea why. So I'd grab my phone and type whatever had been happening in the hours before bed. "Responded to client email while brushing teeth." "Rescheduled lunch meeting during other lunch meeting." "Said yes to leading workshop, felt sick immediately after."

By September I had sixty-three entries. I finally read them all in one sitting, and here's what I saw: almost every single entry contained the phrase "should have" or some variation. I *should have* finished that report yesterday. I *should have* known she'd ask that question. I *shouldn't* need this much sleep. The anxiety wasn't random. It was showing up every single time I'd set an invisible expectation for myself that reality had just violated.

The part that made me feel genuinely stupid? I never once asked whether any of those expectations made sense. I just kept trying to meet them, and when I couldn't, I called it anxiety and looked for ways to manage the feeling instead of questioning the standard.

But here's the thing about managing feelings while leaving the structure intact: you can get really, really good at bailing water and still drown eventually.

That's what this chapter is about. Not managing anxiety better within the life you've already built, but looking at the life itself and asking whether it's something a nervous system can actually sustain. Because if you only ever use regulation tools reactively—when you're already chest-deep in the spiral—you're treating symptoms.

You're putting out fires. And meanwhile, the building's wired wrong.

Most of us don't ask these questions because we're too busy trying to function within the life we have. And a lot of us built that life *while anxious*, which means we built it to accommodate anxiety's demands. The need to stay busy. The need to prove ourselves. The bone-deep certainty that relaxing equals falling behind. The life itself becomes the source of dysregulation—not because you made wrong choices, but because you made them while your nervous system was in a state it was never supposed to sustain long-term.

Let me tell you about Maya, because her story is a clearer illustration than anything I could explain in the abstract.

Maya was a graphic designer at a mid-sized agency in Denver. Twenty-nine. Talented—the kind of designer whose work you'd see and immediately know was hers. Her creative director loved her because she was fast, reliable, and never complained when he dropped urgent projects on her desk at 4 PM on Friday. "Maya will handle it," he'd say, and she always did.

She came to see me because she'd started waking up at 3 AM with her heart pounding so hard she could feel it in her ears. Couldn't fall back asleep. Just lay there in the dark while her brain churned through the next day's task list, re-drafting emails she hadn't sent yet, replaying conversations that hadn't happened. Classic anxiety insomnia. We worked on the usual interventions—cognitive reframing, progressive muscle relaxation, sleep hygiene basics. They helped, somewhat. The 3 AM wake-ups dropped from five nights a week to two or three. But she still described herself as "barely keeping my head above water."

So I asked her to walk me through an average day. Not the aspirational version—the real one.

She started work at 9 AM, officially. But she was checking Slack by 7:30 "just to get ahead of anything urgent." Breakfast was coffee and whatever she could eat while scanning emails. Lunch was fifteen minutes at her desk because taking a real break "felt inefficient." She stayed late most nights—not because anyone explicitly required it, but because "everyone else does and I don't want to look like I'm not committed." She brought her laptop home every evening "just in case." She almost always opened it. Another hour or two after dinner, sometimes more. Weekends were "sort of for me," but she kept notifications on, and when her boss messaged her Saturday afternoon, she'd respond within minutes because "it's easier to just deal with it than let it hang over me."

I said, "That sounds exhausting."

She shrugged. "That's just how it is in creative industries. Everyone's like this."

Here's what I've learned, both professionally and from my own catastrophically slow learning curve: when someone says "that's just how it is," what they're usually describing is a situation they've stopped questioning. And high-functioning anxiety *loves* unquestioned situations, because it gets to write all the rules.

So we started asking different questions. Not "how can I manage my anxiety better within this setup" but "is this setup manageable for a human nervous system at all?"

Turns out: no. Not really.

Here's what became clear over the next few sessions: Maya's job wasn't objectively more demanding than anyone else's at her agency. Her workload was comparable. Her deadlines were tight but not impossible. But she'd built an invisible architecture of self-imposed standards that kept her in a state of perpetual hypervigilance. Respond to every message within ten minutes. Never be the first person to log off for the day. Say yes to every new project, even when her plate was already full. Anticipate problems before anyone else noticed them. Never, ever let anyone see her struggle.

None of those were company policies. They were her own anxious attempts to feel safe by being indispensable. She'd constructed a system where the only way to avoid the fear of being expendable was to never stop performing.

And her body was keeping score.

The real work—the work that actually moved the needle—wasn't learning to breathe through 3 AM panic. It was dismantling the daily architecture that made 3 AM panic inevitable.

She started small. And I mean *small*, because when you're already running on fumes, grand overhauls feel impossible. She turned off Slack notifications before 8 AM and after 6 PM. That's it. One boundary. Ninety minutes in the morning, all evening after six.

First week? She hated it. She felt like she was missing something critical, like she was letting her team down, like she was breaking some unspoken rule that everyone else was following. (She wasn't. No one noticed.) Second week, slightly easier. Her morning coffee tasted better when she wasn't scanning her phone with one hand. Third week, she realized that the urgency she'd been bracing for every morning at 7:30 almost never materialized before 9 anyway. Most of what pinged her early was just people's scattered thoughts, not actual emergencies.

That one tiny shift—reclaiming ninety minutes of her morning and her entire evening from the tyranny of instant availability—didn't fix everything. But it created *space*. Space to eat breakfast sitting down instead of standing at the counter. Space to take an actual lunch break away from her desk, outside, without her phone. Space to sign up for a Wednesday night pottery class, something she used to love in college but had convinced herself she didn't have time for anymore.

And here's the part that genuinely surprised her: her work didn't suffer. She didn't get reprimanded. Her performance reviews stayed strong. The disaster she'd been unconsciously guarding against—the moment when someone would finally realize she wasn't indispensable after all—simply didn't happen.

What did happen was that her 3 AM wake-ups stopped almost entirely within six weeks. Because her nervous system finally had evidence—daily, tangible, repeated evidence—that she could set a boundary and survive it. That she didn't have to be in a constant state of bracing for catastrophe. That maybe, possibly, she could be a competent professional *and* a person with a life outside of work.

Now, you might be thinking: "Sure, but my situation is different. I *actually* have to be available all the time. My boss *actually* expects it. My industry doesn't allow that kind of boundary."

Maybe that's true. Some jobs genuinely are structured to require constant activation—emergency medicine, certain startup phases, crisis management roles. And that's worth examining separately: whether a job that structurally requires you to override your nervous system's signals indefinitely is a job worth keeping.

But more often—and I say this after working with dozens of high-functioning anxious people across wildly different fields—we've conflated "this is how I've been doing it" with "this is the only way it can be done." We've internalized standards that no one actually articulated. We've turned our own preferences for control and safety into absolute requirements. We've mistaken our anxiety's voice for our boss's voice, for industry norms, for reality itself.

And because high-functioning anxiety operates on the core assumption that the only safe position is hypervigilance, we never test those assumptions. We just keep running.

Testing them feels dangerous. I understand that. I spent years—*years*—operating under the belief that if I wasn't constantly producing, constantly available, constantly thinking three steps ahead, I was somehow failing at being a functional adult. Rest felt like a luxury I hadn't earned yet. Downtime felt like stealing. Saying no felt like professional suicide.

The irony, which I can see clearly now but couldn't then: the goalpost for "earned it" kept moving. I never earned rest because the system I'd built didn't allow for earning it. There was always one more thing, one more email, one more client who needed me. The finish line was a mirage.

What finally shifted for me wasn't a single intervention or technique. It was a long, uncomfortable reckoning with what I was actually afraid would happen if I stopped. And when I got honest about it—and this took months, because I'm incredibly good at lying to myself—the answer was this: I was afraid I'd discover I wasn't as competent as I appeared. That my relentless productivity was the only thing making me valuable. That if I slowed down, people would see through the performance and realize I was just anxious and afraid underneath.

That's the fear high-functioning anxiety runs on. Not the fear of failure exactly, though that's part of it. It's the fear of being *revealed*. Of someone finally noticing that you're not as put-together as you seem, that you're barely holding it together, that the competence is a costume you put on every morning and you're terrified it'll slip.

So you stay in motion. Because motion looks like competence. Because stillness feels like exposure. Because if you stop, you'll have to feel what you've been outrunning.

But stillness isn't exposure. Stillness is where you actually hear yourself. And that's exactly what makes it so terrifying—and so necessary.

Building a life that supports sustained regulation isn't about adding more self-care tasks to your already overwhelming to-do list. It's not about scheduling more bubble baths or downloading another meditation app or buying the right supplements. It's about interrogating the structure itself. The scaffolding you've built your days on. What's there because it genuinely matters to you, and what's there because you're trying to outrun a feeling?

Let's get practical, because theory only helps if you can actually use it.

Start by auditing your week. Not in some vague, aspirational way where you mentally gesture toward "being busy." Actually write it down. Track how you're spending your time for five days—weekdays are fine, but if your weekends look completely different, track seven. Include everything. Work tasks, meetings, commute, meals, exercise, screen time, sleep, the hours you spend thinking about work even when you're not technically working. Be honest. No one else has to see this. You're not performing for anyone.

Then look for patterns. Not just "I'm busy"—you already knew that. Look specifically for these things:

Places where you're over-functioning. Tasks you're doing that aren't actually your responsibility, or that you're doing to a standard no one asked for. Emails you're answering at 11 PM that could wait until morning. Projects you've absorbed because saying no felt impossible. Preparation that goes three layers deeper than what's actually required. The gap between what's needed and what you're delivering out of anxiety.

Moments when you're perpetually "on." Times when you're technically resting—watching TV, eating dinner with your partner, sitting on the couch—but your mind is still churning through work. Or you're scrolling your phone. Or you're physically present but mentally three hours ahead, already planning tomorrow, already bracing for the next thing. Your body is sitting still but your nervous system never downshifted.

Absences. Things that used to matter to you but have disappeared from your life entirely. Hobbies you loved. Friendships you've let fade. Movement, play, creativity that isn't monetized or optimized. Actual unstructured downtime where you're not accomplishing anything, not improving yourself, not working toward a goal. Just existing.

Most people, when they actually do this exercise instead of just nodding along, are startled by what they find. Not because they didn't know they were busy—everyone knows they're busy—but because seeing it written out makes the unsustainability undeniable. It's one thing to feel overwhelmed. It's another to see on paper that you worked sixty-three hours last week, slept an average of five and a half hours a night, ate lunch at your desk four out of five days, and spent exactly zero minutes doing something purely because it felt good.

Now here's the harder part: pick *one* thing to change. Not five. Not a complete life overhaul. One.

Because sustainable change doesn't come from a burst of motivation where you decide to transform everything at once and then burn out by Thursday. It comes from small, repeated actions that your nervous system can actually integrate. Changes small enough that your anxiety doesn't immediately throw up every defense mechanism you've got.

Maybe it's a boundary you set. Maybe it's a block of time you reclaim. Maybe it's something you stop doing that you've only been doing out of anxious obligation, out of the fear that if you don't, something terrible will happen.

David—a software engineer I worked with a few years ago—had been running on adrenaline and cold brew for the better part of a decade. Worked for a mid-sized tech company in San Francisco, lived in Oakland, spent about eleven hours a day either working or thinking about work. He came to therapy because his partner had said, gently but seriously, "I feel like I live with a ghost."

His one change: he stopped working weekends. Not because his company forbade it—they didn't care when he worked as long as he hit his sprint goals—but because he realized he was using Saturday and Sunday as a way to manage the chronic low-level panic that he was falling behind.

Except he wasn't falling behind. His velocity was solid. His code reviews were fine. His manager had literally never expressed concern about his output. But the *feeling* of being behind was so constant, so familiar, that he'd stopped questioning whether it was true. He'd just started treating it as reality and organizing his entire life around appeasing it.

The first weekend he didn't work felt excruciating. He described it as "like trying not to scratch a mosquito bite." Twitchy. Guilty. Convinced he was doing something wrong. By Sunday evening he was sure he'd pay for it come Monday morning—that he'd be behind, that people would notice, that he'd regret this.

Monday was fine. Completely fine. No one noticed. No disasters. His sprint started the same as it always did.

Second weekend, slightly easier. Still uncomfortable, still that pull toward his laptop, but less acute. Third weekend, he went hiking with his partner in Marin—something they used to do all the time before work consumed everything. He didn't check his phone once. Came back sunburned and tired and genuinely happy in a way he hadn't felt in months.

Over the course of about three months, something shifted that he hadn't anticipated: he started enjoying his actual life again. Not just tolerating it between work sessions, but genuinely engaging with it. He read fiction—not programming books, actual novels—just because he wanted to. He started cooking elaborate meals on Sunday nights. He remembered that he used to have interests beyond optimizing his productivity, that he used to be a person with curiosity about things that had nothing to do with his career.

And his work? Still good. Still reliable. Still met every deadline. But it was no longer the only thing determining whether he was okay on any given day.

This isn't about work-life balance, by the way. I've come to genuinely hate that phrase because it implies that work and life are separate, opposing forces you're trying to equilibrate, like you're a scale with professional achievement on one side and personal fulfillment on the other and you're trying to keep the thing level.

That's not how it works. Your work is part of your life. And if it's structured in a way that requires you to constantly override your body's signals—hunger, fatigue, the need for connection, the need for rest—just to keep up, that's not a balance problem. That's a design problem.

And you can't regulate your way out of fundamentally dysregulating circumstances.

Let's talk about rest for a minute, because I think we've culturally obliterated any functional understanding of what that word actually means.

Rest is not the same as collapse. It's not what you do after you've already burned yourself out and you physically can't continue. It's not a reward you earn by working hard enough or being productive enough. It's not scrolling your phone in bed because you're too tired to do anything else but not actually relaxed enough to sleep.

Rest is a basic biological necessity, like water or oxygen. And treating it as optional—or as something you have to justify, something you only deserve after you've earned it—is how you end up with a nervous system that's forgotten how to downregulate.

Real rest means doing something, or doing nothing, without any agenda attached to it. Not resting so you can be more productive tomorrow. Not resting because you finally hit some arbitrary milestone and now you've "earned" it. Resting because you're a human being with a body that needs it to function, and no amount of optimization or willpower changes that fact.

I know how that sounds. Indulgent, maybe. Naive, definitely, in a world that doesn't exactly slow down for anyone. But consider what happens when you don't rest—when you treat rest as optional or weak or something other people need but you've somehow transcended.

Your body stays in a state of activation. Your cortisol levels don't drop. Your sleep suffers, which means your emotional regulation suffers, which means your digestion suffers, your immune system suffers, your ability to think clearly suffers. You become more reactive. More irritable. More prone to exactly the kind of anxious spirals we've been talking about for eight chapters now. You're not being virtuous by pushing through. You're accumulating a debt that your body will eventually collect on, with interest.

I learned this the hard way, which seems to be the only way I learn anything important.

A few years ago—this would've been 2021, middle of the pandemic—I spent about six months in what I can only describe as chronic low-grade burnout. I was still functional. Still seeing clients, still meeting deadlines, still showing up to things. But I felt like I was operating from behind a pane of glass. Everything was distant. Muted. I'd be in session with a client and part of my brain would be somewhere else entirely, just watching myself go through the motions. My sleep was terrible—not insomnia exactly, but that shallow, restless kind of sleep where you're never quite sure if you actually slept or just lay there thinking for eight hours. My patience was nonexistent. I snapped at my partner over things that didn't matter. I kept getting these tension headaches that no amount of ibuprofen would touch, just this low constant pressure behind my eyes.

A friend finally asked me, "When's the last time you took a day off where you didn't do anything productive?"

I couldn't remember. Legitimately couldn't remember.

So I tried it. Cleared a Saturday—no clients, no emails, no catching up on clinical notes or reading journal articles or any of the seventeen things I'd been telling myself I needed to do. Drove out to Point Reyes, walked down to the beach, and just sat there. Watched the waves. Let my mind wander. Didn't document it for social media, didn't try to make it meaningful or transformative, didn't turn it into content. Just sat on the sand and existed.

It was genuinely excruciating for the first hour. My brain kept trying to assign me tasks. *You should be working on that article. You're wasting time. This is pointless. You could be getting so much done right now.* The voice was relentless.

But I stayed. And eventually—maybe an hour in, maybe longer—the noise started to quiet. I felt something I hadn't felt in months, maybe longer: actually present. Not thinking about what I needed to do later, not replaying a session from earlier that week, not planning or analyzing or optimizing. Just there. In my body. Watching the ocean move.

That one day didn't fix everything. I didn't come back transformed. But it reminded me of something I'd completely forgotten: I'm allowed to exist without producing anything. My worth isn't contingent on my output. And my nervous system, given half a chance, actually knows how to rest—I'd just stopped giving it permission.

Here's what I want you to try, if nothing else from this chapter lands: schedule one hour this week—put it in your calendar like you would a meeting—where you do something that has absolutely no purpose other than the fact that it feels good. Not exercise because it's healthy. Not reading because it's educational. Not networking because it's strategic. Something completely useless by any productivity metric.

Play a video game. Sit in a park and watch dogs. Bake something you're not going to photograph. Listen to an entire album start to finish without multitasking. Lie on the floor and stare at the ceiling. Whatever sounds appealing in a way that has nothing to do with self-improvement.

And notice what comes up for you. Notice if guilt shows up, or restlessness, or that voice that insists this is a waste of time and you should be doing something more important. Don't fight those feelings. Don't try to regulate them away. Just notice them. Observe them like you're a scientist watching a really interesting specimen.

Because that voice—that restless, guilty voice insisting you shouldn't be resting—is your anxiety. It's the part of you that's convinced your value is tied to your productivity, that stopping is dangerous, that you have to earn the right to exist. And it's wrong. But you won't know it's wrong until you practice doing the thing anyway and see that nothing terrible happens.

Connection matters too, though we almost never talk about it in the context of anxiety regulation. Humans are wired for co-regulation. That's not pop psychology—it's basic neurobiology. Our nervous systems literally calm down in the presence of safe others. When you're with someone who sees you, who isn't asking you to perform or prove anything, your body registers that as safety. Your heart rate slows. Your breathing deepens. The chronic tension you've been carrying starts to ease, not because you did a technique, but because you're not alone in your activation.

But high-functioning anxiety drives us toward isolation. Because isolation feels safer than vulnerability. If no one gets too close, no one can see the cracks. If you keep moving, keep achieving, keep the performance going, you never have to admit that you're struggling.

Except isolation doesn't actually help you regulate. It just means you're struggling alone. It means the only voice you hear is your own anxious one, and that voice is not a reliable narrator.

Think about who in your life you can be *real* with. Not the polished version of yourself. Not the competent high-achiever who has it all together. The person who's tired and scared and doesn't have answers. The person who sometimes wakes up at 3 AM convinced they're failing at everything.

If that list is short—or if it's nonexistent—that's worth addressing. Not because there's something wrong with you, but because trying to sustain regulation without any relational support is like trying to build a house without a foundation. You can do it, technically. It's just precarious as hell and it won't hold up under pressure.

I'm not suggesting you need a huge social circle. You don't. One or two people who genuinely get you, who you can text when you're spiraling and who won't try to fix you or minimize what you're feeling or tell you it's not that bad—that's enough. That's actually enormous.

And if you don't have that right now, therapy counts. A good therapist can be that person for you while you're building or rebuilding other connections. There's zero shame in that. I've been on both sides of it—as the therapist obviously, but also as the client, sitting in someone else's office at 32 years old trying to articulate feelings I'd spent a decade avoiding because admitting I was struggling felt like admitting I was weak.

It helped. Not because my therapist gave me answers or fixed me, but because she gave me space to stop pretending I was fine. And that space—just having one hour a week where I didn't have to perform competence—made it possible to start being honest with other people too.

One more thing, and I mean this: you're going to have days where none of this works. Where you set the boundaries, where you rest, where you reach out, where you do all the things we've talked about across nine chapters, and you still feel like you're drowning. Where your chest is tight and your thoughts won't stop spiraling and you're convinced you're doing everything wrong.

That's not failure. That's being human.

Regulation isn't a state you achieve and then maintain forever like some kind of enlightenment. It's a practice. Some days the practice feels easy, almost automatic. You notice the activation early, you use the tools, your nervous system responds, you come back to baseline. Other days it's a slog. You're white-knuckling your way through, the tools feel like they're not working, and you end the day exhausted from the effort of just staying functional.

Both of those days are part of the process. What matters is that you keep coming back to it. That you don't use one hard day—or one hard week—as evidence that you're broken or that nothing works. You're not broken. You're learning to live in a way your body can actually sustain instead of the way your anxiety has been demanding, and that learning curve isn't linear. It never is.

The life you're building—the one that actually supports you instead of constantly depleting you—doesn't happen in one grand transformation. It happens in small, repeated choices that feel insignificant in the moment but compound over time.

The choice to set a boundary even when it feels uncomfortable, even when you're not sure you're "allowed" to. The choice to rest even when your brain insists you haven't earned it yet. The choice to reach out to someone instead of isolating and trying to handle everything alone. The choice to question whether the pace you're keeping is actually necessary, or just familiar. The choice to stop treating your anxiety's voice as objective truth about reality.

Those choices feel small. On any given Tuesday, setting one boundary or taking one real lunch break or sending one honest text to a friend doesn't feel like it's changing anything. But those small choices compound. Slowly. Quietly. In ways you might not notice day to day.

But over weeks and months, they add up to a life where anxiety is something you experience occasionally instead of something you're organizing your entire existence around. Where you can be competent *and* human. Driven *and* rested. Successful *and* soft. Where you don't have to choose between being functional and being okay.

You don't have to keep running. You never did. The thing you've been racing toward—the point where you'll finally feel safe, where you'll finally be enough, where you can finally stop—doesn't exist out there in the future. It's not waiting for you after one more achievement or one more accomplishment or one more proof that you're worthy.

It's here. Right now. In the choice to stop organizing your life around anxiety's demands and start building something your actual self can live in.

So what happens when you do stop? When you've built a life with enough space that you finally slow down and feel what you've been outrunning—not just the surface anxiety, but the deeper stuff underneath? The beliefs about worthiness, about safety, about what you have to do to deserve to exist? When you've created enough sustained regulation that your defenses start to relax and you see what's been there all along, waiting for you to turn around and look at it?

That's where things get interesting. And by interesting, I mean uncomfortable in a way that catches most people completely off guard.

Because here's what no one tells you about building better regulation skills: they work. They really do work. Your nervous system starts to trust that it can downshift. The constant background hum of activation starts to quiet. And when it does, when you're not using all your energy just to stay functional, you start noticing things you've been too busy to feel.

Grief that's been waiting. Anger you didn't have permission to acknowledge. Loneliness that all the achievement was supposed to fix but never quite did. The quiet, persistent question you've been drowning out with motion: *Is this actually what I want, or just what I thought I was supposed to want?*

Most people expect that building a sustainable life will feel like relief. And it does, eventually. But first, it often feels like everything you've been holding together is starting to fall apart. Not because you're doing it wrong—because you're finally doing it right, and right means feeling what you've been running from.

What you do with those feelings, how you meet them, whether you let them teach you something or whether you panic and sprint back toward the familiar chaos of overfunction—that's the real work. And it doesn't fit neatly into a chapter on sustaining regulation, because it's bigger than regulation. It's about what becomes possible when you're not spending all your energy just trying to survive your own life.

But that's a different conversation. For now, start with the small stuff. The one boundary. The one hour of useless rest. The one honest conversation. Start there, and see what happens. See what your life starts to feel like when you're building it for a person, not a performance.

You might be surprised by who that person turns out to be.

Also in the Series

Every book in Anxiety Reset stands on its own — read them in any order. If this one was useful, the library continues:

Anxiety for No Reason

Nighttime Anxiety

The Anxious Achiever

Anxiety in Public

Anticipatory Anxiety

Anxiety and the Overthinking Loop

Anxiety After a Panic Attack

Also in the Series

www.ingramcontent.com/pod-product-compliance
Lightning Source LLC
LaVergne TN
LVHW010720061126
851857LV00014B/1280
* 9 7 8 1 8 0 4 2 8 3 3 3 2 *